THE ESSENTIAL PROFESSION:
Contemporary Issues in Education

THE ESSENTIAL PROFESSION:
Contemporary Issues in Education

Edited by Marvin B. Scott

GREYLOCK PUBLISHERS
Stamford, Conn.

Printed in the United States of America.
Library of Congress Catalog Card Number: 75-40862.
ISBN: 0-89223-044-4 (soft cover).
        0-89223-045-2 (hard cover).

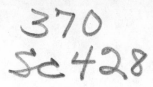
*For three influential women in my life of learning
who would have been proud of this book.*

*Dr. Bronnetta L. Scott,
Mrs. Lottie Taylor Brown,
and
Mrs. Almeta Lewis*

CONTENTS

PREFACE

Education today reflects the complexity of modern society. It is also charged with preparing young people to cope with this complexity. The profession is in a pivotal position in the mid 1970s. Its detractors hold it responsible for a variety of contemporary problems, its supporters point to positive innovations, while all agree as to its essential role in shaping our society.

Persons considering a career in education should be made aware of the issues and challenges awaiting them. Accountability, testing, special education, bilingualism, media technology, career education, and desegregation are all integral to teaching and learning. These are not new issues and challenges, but they demand new considerations and responses.

This book presents fresh and comprehensive analyses of contemporary educational issues. Each essay was written by a prominent specialist in his or her field, and completed late in 1975, thus assuring up to date perspectives. The book will be of special interest to students in introductory education courses, as well as to teachers and administrators anxious to stay informed of critical trends. There are very few "answers" here, very few solemn pronouncements as to what's wrong and what can be done. Instead, the editor and essayists agreed that the book should pose the sorts of questions that demand serious and motivated consideration.

Serious and motivated teachers will be needed in the coming years. In addition to the more somber aspects of the profession, the joys and rewards are represented here too. The book seeks to encourage young people to become teachers. The challenges are formidable, but those anxious to meet them will find great and lasting satisfaction. Very few professions touch so many people in so many crucial ways.

Marvin B. Scott

I.

WHY TEACH?

By Marvin B. Scott

For many of you this will be your first contact with a professional course in education. It may either enhance your interest in the profession or cause you to beat a hasty retreat into the liberal arts.

Some of you have chosen the teaching profession because a parent or other relative has been a teacher. Some of you have been inspired by an elementary or high school teacher who demonstrated what a good teacher really is. There are others of you who are following the long tradition of moving, via the education ladder, from the blue-collar trades. A few of you may have decided to enter the profession almost by default, as a way of gaining insurance against not succeeding in other fields. Such students tend to regard the teaching profession as a profession of the last resort. Sometimes they have started in a college of liberal arts, but they have not been successful there. Indeed, they have found few academic areas that meet their needs. These few students do neither themselves nor their colleges of education a service.

Teaching demands the best minds. The underlying goal of education is to develop to the fullest possible extent the capabilities of each and every pupil. A strong commitment to the profession is absolutely necessary if such a goal is to be achieved. Teaching requires commitment and dedication and, often, a willingness to forego the greater financial rewards offered by some other professions.

Who is to teach, then? What does the future hold, and if a commitment is made to the profession, is there a chance for continued employment? How can one make a decision to teach when the present job market is so limited? This chapter will attempt to answer these and some other questions which are essential to an adequate understanding and appreciation of the profession.

Teachers played an important part in the formation of this country. They participated significantly in forming its value structure and have contributed greatly to the transmission and acculturation of ideas and ideals. For a long time teachers held a high position in American society, almost to the point of being exalted in some communities. Today, the profession itself is facing some hard realities which affect in-service, as well as prospective teachers.

The post World War II "baby boom" created a need for thousands of new teachers. This increase in the size of the national student body had not been anticipated adequately. As a result, many poorly trained teachers entered the profession. An emphasis on quantity sacrificed quality and led to a helter-skelter development of schools of education. This generation is suffering the excesses of that period. Schools of education are now faced with dwindling numbers of students and substantially reduced programs. The baby boom is over, and school systems are seeing gradual but steady reductions in the size of pupil enrollments. As a matter of fact, the entire labor market is strained and those who finish college are no longer certain to find a preferred job. Some PhD's are pumping gas. There is stiff competition at the highest levels among those with the most impressive credentials. The situation is far worse for the country's minority groups; America is still not providing equal training and opportunity for all its citizens.

What are the answers? We can begin by examining the needs and priorities of the country and by establishing a sense of reality about hoped for outcomes. Teachers will play a vital part in this endeavor. They will train a group of Americans, and instill in them a sense of equality which has not existed heretofore in this country.

Problems

If you are serious about being part of the teaching profession you must understand that it has problems, as do all professions. Today the field is crowded with those who have prepared for a career which does not have positions for them, as well as with some who were not trained for the teaching positions they hold. In today's terminology that is called "teacher oversupply." The extent of that oversupply is indicated by the following statistic.

The number of college graduates will exceed the number of jobs requiring their skills by about 800,000 between now and 1985, according to projections from the Department of Labor's Bureau of Labor Statistics....Overall the Bureau estimates that

15.3 million people with B.A. or higher degrees will be looking for jobs over the period from 1972 to 1985. The total includes 11.2 million new bachelor's-degree recipients, 1.2 million new M.A.'s, 770,000 new recipients of doctorates or first professional degrees, and 2.1 million delayed entrants with college-level training—women who decide to enter the job market after several years of domestic life and persons leaving military service to look for civilian jobs. Over the same period the Bureau predicts, 14.5 million jobs requiring college-level training will be available....The projected "gap" between supply and demand will be greater after 1980 than before....Until 1980, the job deficit will total about 12,500 a year. Between 1980 and 1985, it will increase to 140,000 a year....The overall projections show oversupply in such fields as: chemistry, food science, geology, history, law, life science, meteorology, oceanography, physics, political science, and elementary and secondary education.[1]

One way to address this problem in the teaching field would be to reduce the number of people training to be teachers by raising the standards of admission to colleges of education. This approach has been supported by many educators for a number of years in the hope that more stringent admission criteria would eventually improve the quality of education being offered in the country's school systems. Such an approach has obvious faults, however, including a possible further exclusion of members of the various minority groups. Instead, universities and colleges are now preparing new and more varied programs. Future instructors will reflect these programs and bring to the classroom more responsive and appropriate instruction, based on the needs and capabilities of all. We must ensure at the college level that our best minds receive our best training. There will never be an oversupply of excellent teachers.

The financial rewards of teaching are meager. The average teacher's salary in this country is lower than that of a trash collector in many large cities and lower than that of many police officers. The average teacher makes approximately $11,000 a year. What would that mean in terms of meeting monthly expenses? It would mean that if you were unmarried and a beginning professional, you could afford a small apartment, a small car, some clothes, sufficient but not elaborate food, taxes, and a basic amount of everything else: health care, personal care, reading, music, entertainment, etc. If you were very careful, you might be able to save as much as $50 a month. Teaching is not a career in which to earn great wealth. However, the question of income must not be overemphasized in a profession that calls for truly dedicated individuals.

In the past, some teacher colleges appeared to operate on the premise that a limited amount of academic preparation was enough to equip teachers for their careers. Even today, the standards of performance asked of some teachers-in-training are not as high as they should be. A graduating senior recently said that his practice teaching experience had been both silly and irrelevant. How could this happen today? Those of us in the profession must take responsibility for such inadequacies, of training. Many professional schools prepare students poorly for the world of work and schools of education are no exception.

[1]*The Chronicle of Higher Education.* "A Glut of College Graduates?" Vol. X, No. 5, 1975, pp. 1 and 8.

During the decade of the sixties schools of education came to grips with theory and practice and endeavored to train students in field settings related to employment opportunities. It is still true that some schools of education do not have enough well-trained staff to give the kind of supervision needed for truly rewarding practice teaching. But this is changing as practice teaching receives a more appropriate emphasis.

When our cities were first developing, teachers lived near their schools and could participate in the affairs of the community. That is frequently not the case today. Inner-city teachers often live great distances from where they teach and often have little or no contact with parents or the community around the school. Contact with parents is limited to questions or problems having to do with a particular child. But here again, change is taking place. Many teachers are discovering that certain regulations compel them to live in the communities that employ them.

It is important for teachers to understand their constituents, their pupils and their families, and the community within which they live. Neighborhood schools were built around this idea. It is tragic that the concept of neighborhood schools has come to be used as a weapon by those who oppose integration of schools. As more teachers settle in the communities where they work, then the teaching profession will begin to regain the high standing it used to enjoy. Teachers will also become more effective in the classroom and more sensitive to the needs of the children. Some school systems are still afflicted with nepotism or favoritism. Some school boards do not meet the needs of their clients, the students, and some do not have the qualifications to make the necessary decisions in a reasoned and intelligent way. There are some politicians who prey on the educational system of our country for their personal political ends.

Despite the problems which have been touched on here, interest in the field of teaching has remained high. Each year more and more students enter college with the intention of teaching at the elementary or secondary level. The motivation of these students is well intended and the profession is in need of this interest and vitality. At the same time, this motivation needs to be effectively utilized. It is essential that the right teacher ends up in the right school and is effective at what she or he is doing. Energy and commitment can be sustained by early identification of strong interests and abilities. Counseling procedures can help prospective teachers focus and concentrate on those things which they do best. Experienced educators can contribute by defining what the profession needs and what kinds of people make the best teachers. Programs designed to complement a student's strengths and interest will assure both a high degree of involvement as a student and competence as a teacher.

Challenges

Problems become challenges when they are confronted. If every classroom has an excellent teacher in it, problems of low standing, over-supply, meager income, lacks in professional training, or any other pro-blem would either not exist or would be well on the way towards solu-tion.

How, then, can teachers be helped to become more competent? How can they best capitalize on the skills they acquire in training? Com-petence in any field is made evident by performance. Therefore, we must develop ways to observe and classify the performance of teachers in specific learning settings. Performance in this case is de-fined as the ability of an instructor first to diagnose the conditions most conducive to maximum realization of a child's potential for learn-ing and then to provide this learning situation. This kind of competent performance will be maintained if teachers are constantly updating their own professional education. A teacher with several years experience might well be looking for new techniques, additional knowledge, previously unexplored insights and many other resources with which to extend and expand his or her teaching capabilities. Having taught for a while, this teacher is now aware of certain needs. Opportunities for con-tinuing education must become more widespread and frequent. It is a hopeful sign that some school systems are now requiring their teachers to go back to school, on a continuing basis to improve their skills and in-crease their knowledge. The competent classroom teacher will become the hallmark of our profession if we demand excellence and supply the methods by which it can be both achieved and sustained.

Self-knowledge is vital for success in teaching, and so is self-control. For instance, if you plan to become a classroom teacher, examine yourself as a person most carefully. Discover your biases, your strengths, your weaknesses, your reactions to a variety of situations. Self-awareness will enable you to be in command of yourself and that in turn will make it possible for you to give of yourself as a teacher.

Once you have begun to understand yourself, and this will be an on-going process, then your capacity for understanding and appreciating others will increase. Relating to other people is a critical teaching skill. Skills of interaction are learned both formally and informally and they lend vitality to teaching. Finally, awareness of yourself and of the people around you will enable you to look at the larger environments which af-fect all of us; our city, our state, our country, our world. Expanded awareness will make your performance in the classroom alive and pro-ductive.

Teachers are expected to pass on to the youth of this society the techniques and values that will make the learner able to participate in a democratic society. Teachers-to-be must be alert to the needs of society and be prepared to interpret them for their students. Current societal needs are highly varied and will challenge your imagination. Some of the needs are discussed in this book: bilingual education, special education, career education, integrated education, and continuing education. It is important to keep the teaching profession in the forefront of social change so that those who are educated in our schools are fully prepared to be part of their individual communities and of our national community.

To sum up, this is how a newspaper columnist views the problems and challenges in education today.

We are raising a nation of 'culturally disadvantaged' children

James J. Kilpatrick

The College Entrance Examination Board released its analysis of 1975 test results a few days ago. The figures were shocking, dismaying, disturbing—pick your adjective—but they were not surprising.

Any experienced educator, any newspaper editor, any personnel director could have predicted the dismal report: Test scores last spring dropped for the 12th consecutive year. The Class of '75 scored 10 points lower in verbal skills and eight points lower in mathematical skills than the high school graduates of the preceding year. The average scores were the lowest in two decades.

There is a defensive tendency, in certain liberal circles, to explain the decline in terms of the increasing number of "culturally disadvantaged" students who take the tests every year. The theory holds that the tests are "culturally biased," but the theory is specious. The standardized tests are based upon verbal and mathematical skills that should be within the grasp of any high school graduate applying for college entrance. In any event, the increasing numbers of such disadvantaged pupils are not significant in a test group of nearly a million students.

What we have here is disaster. Perhaps the most disheartening figures have to do with the 20 percent decline in the number of students scoring at superior levels on the verbal test. This test measures simple literacy—the ability to read, to write, to understand, and to communicate. These are fundamental skills, on which all else depends. It is bad enough that mathematical skills are dropping; we are raising children who cannot make change, double a recipe, measure board-feet, or calculate miles per gallon. It is worse to

raise a generation unable to read and to follow the instructions on a box.

The melancholy situation is familiar to every person whose work brings him close to high school graduates. There are exceptions, of course—brilliant exceptions—but today's typical graduate is in deep trouble. After 12 years of schooling, he misspells even the easy words; he cannot read fluently aloud; he makes a mere stab at punctuation; he stumbles over the elementary questions of an application form.

The University of Wisconsin recently gave a test on English usage to students intending to take up journalism. Of 200 who took the test, 125 flunked. The failure rate was double the 30 percent of a year ago. And these were students who want to be writers!

Over this past weekend, various observers fumbled to explain the college entrance scores. Technology was to blame: We no longer write letters, we talk on the telephone instead; we no longer read newspapers attentively, we rely on TV. Some observers mentioned the disruptions of school desegregation. Between 1955 and 1975, we were reminded, high school students lived through a time of disenchantment, tension, and national unease; they could not concentrate.

Well, maybe. It occurs to me that the primary blame for this colossal failure should be placed squarely upon the educational establishment. Our schools have been afflicted with teachers more interested in fads than in fundamentals. The textbook publishing houses, obsessed with form instead of substance, bear a terrible burden of guilt. The taxpayers have invested a fortune in their schools and the investment has been frittered away. The teachers' unions are striking for more, more, more.

When we look at their end products, the graduates of '75, let us ask why, why, why?

I was reared in the public schools of Oklahoma City. We had spelling bees; we wrote weekly themes; we diagrammed sentences; we were made to memorize great chunks of Longfellow, Poe, Wordsworth, and Shakespeare. We were blessed with teachers who loved to teach, teachers who were not preoccupied with the check-off, the union shop, fringe benefits, and enforcement of the seven-hour day.

The situation will not improve. Millions of school children are today being cheated out of a solid, basic education, but the pity is that they only dimly perceive what they are missing. As their own children grow up, and new teachers come along, standards will steadily diminish. Let us look at these test scores and weep for the "culturally disadvantaged." We are raising a nation of them.

James J. Kilpatrick is a syndicated columnist.

Boston Globe, September 18, 1975.

This is a conservative viewpoint, but it does describe the attitudes and concerns of a great many Americans. The challenges of the teaching profession demand creativity and knowledge. As you prepare to be excellent teachers, think about the attitudes and concerns described above and the extent to which you feel a commitment to respond to them.

Why Teach?

This question is one you may have asked yourself many times. Some of the factors that influenced your decision were described earlier. In a sense, everyone is a teacher. We all ask and answer questions and share information. We constantly learn; we seem to do this at all ages and under all sorts of conditions. Learning is a continuing process, and teaching is a continuing and essential factor in learning.

More teachers will be needed in the next 20 years as the school age population increases slightly. But a larger quantity of teachers by itself will not serve well either the increased number of learners or the teaching profession. A new breed of teacher is required, and one seems to be developing. This new kind of teacher could be called a multiprofessional: one who has expertise in several fields and who is able to impart knowledge with joy and strength.

One of the joys of teaching is seeing the smiles of learners when they achieve mastery of new skills. An even greater joy is watching students acquire a degree of self-understanding and self-awareness which they had not had prior to becoming part of the learning situation. Teaching provides a feeling of accomplishment just from being on the job. Being a teacher can almost fill you with awe: your mistakes will haunt you for the rest of your life; and your accomplishments will stand as testimony to your constant efforts to provide excellent education.

It is clear that the teaching profession can and will coexist with other areas of professional studies simply because it lies at the heart of every other endeavor. The teaching profession is the essential profession. The personal rewards and joys gained by being part of this essential profession will continue to remain high.

We hope you will thoughtfully set your goals and consider carefully your choice of teaching as a profession. The caution lights are many, and they should be duly observed as you move ahead in your training. Remember, though, that they are just caution signals; they are not road blocks. Think about teaching and your reasons for entering the profession. Think about what you hope to be able to offer your future students as well as what you can offer the profession. Think about the unique and exciting process of opening minds to the whole world of knowledge. And then, go teach!

II.

ACCOUNTABILITY: A Blessing or an Affliction?

By Roland E. Barnes

Before 1970 the term accountability did not appear in educational reference books. Not until 1968 was there an official requirement (of two federal programs) that educators be held accountable for pre-stated learnings of students. Prior to 1969 and 1970 the stance of the education profession was that students should be held accountable for their learnings. It was this shift of claim as to who was accountable for students' learnings that spawned the current issues of accountability in education.

Two major conditions of long standing favored the arousal of attention to accountability. First, continually increasing costs and taxes for education caused intensive examination of what returns resulted from expenditures and how efficiently funds were being utilized. Extensive data about costs of resources provided for education could be documented. However, little hard data could be presented about results of learning on the part of students. Various management processes from business, industry, and government were utilized in attempts to remedy this lack. Still the actual results of learning remained elusive. Second, continuing dissatisfaction with schools and their failure with many children and youth caused citizens to question teachers and administrators about instruction. Reports of most federally funded programs indicated that after massive infusion of monies performance levels had remained the same or declined. The drop-out rate among students continually rose. Minorities, the disadvantaged, and the poor clamored for adequate learning for their children. The push for quality education became a national subject in an education message in 1970 by then president Nixon.

In the interim since 1970 there is still widespread interest in the concept of accountability, but little progress in applying it to the educational enterprise. While no one expresses opposition to the concept of accountability there is much public debate about the current formulation of accountability that has been advanced since 1969-70.

This essay is an attempt to examine the concept of accountability to differentiate its blessings and afflictions as it is currently formulated and as it may ultimately develop.

The Current Formulation of Accountability

The application of the concept of accountability to the education enterprise is borrowed from the field of business management. It assumes that in education there is a product, such as the end-product in a business operation (a refrigerator, a suit, a car, etc.). The end-product in education is viewed as "what the student learns". The major emphasis focuses on the *performance* of the student *on pre-determined, specific objectives.* Proof of performance is accomplished by sources external to the school system through an audit which is reported publicly. Compensation is paid for accomplishing objectives, reduced for failure to attain objectives, and a premium added for exceeding stated objectives. Performance objectives have been limited to statements capable of precise measurement, usually in the basic skills of reading and arithmetic, that utilize scores on standardized tests. Larger objectives and those that are difficult to define and measure have not been included in current efforts to implement accountability operations. In sum, the broad concept of accountability seems to have been narrowed operationally to what is commonly termed *performance contracting.* A formal contract is entered into (usually with a business organization external to the school system) to increase student performance by a stated number of grade levels during a specified time period and for a specified cost. It is in the aspect of implementing a policy or plan for accountability in school systems that major problems arise.

Problems in Implementing an Accountability Concept

Prior to the mid-1960s accountability was assumed in our society but was seldom made definite or specific. Guarantees, and warranties on products were often so indefinite or full of loopholes that they meant little for holding the manufacturer accountable for the product. During the past 10 years there has been extensive growth of consumerism, which is a form of accountability protection. The consumer expects that a product purchased will render proper service under proper use over some specific time period. If the product fails to do this then the manufacturer is obligated to repair or replace the product.

In industry the product is usually an object, simple or complex, which is easily amenable to quality checks and which can be tested under actual conditions of use to determine that it does or does not perform satisfactorily. However, it has only been during the past ten years that the public has clamored for the satisfactory performance of products. In the past the efficiency of a business was measured in profit and loss rather than in the performance of its product.

It is significant that the current formulation of accountability in education attempts to utilize business and industrial processes to measure the output of instruction, that output not being an object but the complex phenomenon we call learning. The setting for the product of learning is not a plant which uses materials that meet certain specifications when they are delivered. The setting is a school where human beings of diverse ages, backgrounds of experience, abilities, and motivations come together. In the plant or factory the raw materials are controlled and processed through known stages until the desired product results. In the school the human beings respond to and interact with the controls and processes utilized, so that unlike the materials used in a factory, there is no assurance that all will behave or be formed exactly alike. By now it should be obvious to the reader that one of the major problems in accountability in education is the misapplication of business management procedures to a function that is vastly different from a business or industrial operation. This should not be construed as precluding the application of accountability to the education enterprise. It does imply that educational accountability needs to be developed as related to the purposes and expectations about learning. These are not as finite and easy to assess as are the products of a plant or factory.

Keeping in mind that some new form of accountability in education should be developed, it is helpful to explore some of the problems in formulating policy and implementing accountability in education. The major problem areas deal with (1) the goals of education, (2) the objectives of education, their measurement and evaluation, and (3) who should be held accountable for what.

In order to implement any system of accountability it is imperative that a school system express commitment to a set of broad goals for what is to be expected from education in that local community. Stated another way, the local community must say clearly what shall be the purposes of education in its schools. Unfortunately, in most school systems in this country there never has been a consensus of what shall be the goals of education. The various publics in a local school community hold divergent expectations about what schools should do. School administrators and teachers frequently find themselves in the seething cauldron of diverse expectations. School boards seem to move with the tide of whatever groups bring most pressure to bear at any one time. Seldom are forums established in the community to attempt to arrive at some consensus about what should be the purposes of education. Few state departments of education have exercised leadership in encouraging local school districts to adopt and utilize goals in planning and decision-making. The federal government has caused the adoption of some goals through its categorical grants in programs such as the National Defense Education, Elementary and Secondary, and Emergency School Assistance Acts.

The governance of education as a state function through local school districts (except in Hawaii) creates a peculiar "politics of education" separate from the usual two-party politics of other local government. With no party machinery available for reaching compromise before elections, major disagreements spill over onto the local school board which must contend with diverse and conflicting demands of the various publics in a school system. Each of these publics expects and demands that the school board adopt its point of view. School board members frequently are elected because of a promise to support the particular views of some group. This political process seldom results in efforts to achieve some consensus about what shall be the purposes of education.

The various publics or groups in a local school system contain individuals who hold similar views about what schools should do in educating students. These individuals value certain qualities they feel should be developed through education. They possess an image of the educated person they expect the schools to produce. They are sure of the attitudes, skills and abilities that education should foster. Philosophers tell us there are at least five different views of the ideal type of educated person which can become models for the school to produce. Considerable difficulty arises around goals because (1) publics are not always clear about which model they desire and (2) we have not developed the means to measure the success, or lack of it, of learning based on a particular model.

Further, one's view of the educated child shapes his conception of what knowledge is important. In following one view and emphasizing its particular kind of knowledge one cannot escape slighting the conceptions of knowledge important to another view. How then does a school or a school system agree on goals that accomodate all of the five or more basic views of what makes the educated person?

Still another hindrance to agreeing on goals for education is the lack of agreement about what shall be the role of the schools in our society. In any single school district there are persons who hold views along this entire continuum of what may be the school's role: (1) schools should not be involved in social change—they should be isolated from social matters; (2) schools recognize social change but should not engage directly in those matters—students should look at current matters by examining what great men have said about those conditions; (3) schools should take an active role in social change—the changeable nature of human experience is emphasized as are the problem-solving approaches the student must use to exist; (4) schools themselves should be agencies of social change and become leaders for implementing change; (5) schools should negate the scoial reality of human existence—persons may define themselves through other than social reality. Hence, one's view of the role of the school in society also shapes the kind of goal statements that would be acceptable.

Referring back to the section of this essay on "The Current Formulation of Accountability," it should be quite clear that a broader, more inclusive set of considerations regarding accountability needs to be derived. The current formulation focuses on a single view of implicit goals that fail to accomodate the diverse views of persons that make up our society. Further, specific objectives of learning need to be extracted from stated (not implicit) goals which every group or public in a school district has participated in developing. With the diverse and often conflicting views of groups and individuals about (1) the purposes of schools, (2) the model of the educated person, (3) the knowledge that is important, and (4) the role of the schools, arriving at agreement about goal statements becomes time-consuming. It also requires leadership and negotiating skills on the part of school board members, professional educators, citizens and students. It is an aspect of education in which citizens should take the lead and predominate. Only when a local community is able to state what its goals for education are can it begin to establish accountability for the results of what those goals explicate. This is where policy and design of an accountability system must begin.

From the stated goals of education we derive the specific objectives for attaining the knowledges, skills, abilities, attitudes, feelings and behaviors related to a particular goal. This is not a problem and many school systems across the country have accomplished this. The problem arises in the current formulation of accountability that requires only specific objectives that can be measured by test (usually standardized ones) in the basic skills or subjects. The result is an emphasis on the concrete and specific to the detriment of other equally important components of education. It also results in diminished value for subjects like art and music. It eventually would result in limiting "education to the point where whatever could not be measured could not be taught,"as stated by Girard D. Hottleman in his article for *The Massachusetts Teacher*.

A big can of worms is exposed by the limited measures of achievement that characterize the current formulation of accountability. It is claimed that these limited measures are justified because reading and math are skill subjects and we must start with measures that already exist. It tends to narrow the educational function to primarily basic cognitive. The artistic, affective and the attitudinal become secondary, at best. It seems to reward unreflective habit formation rather than developing habits of inquiry.

In addition, the use of a limited set of specific objectives that can be measured by tests reduces the learner to a passive party in the teaching-learning process. It assumes that the teacher is able to control all the variables in the learning processes of the student. It makes no allowance for the unpredictable actions that may occur in an instructional situation.

An extensive range of measures needs to be developed in order to assess the full range of learnings that occur in school. These measures need to guage not only in relation to some norm, such as in standardized tests, but also relative to individual attainment. Some measures should be of a nature that students may apply them to judge results without help of the teacher. Other measures need to be used to assess behaviors both in and out of school through data collected from many sources and persons. Such things as critical thinking, creativity, self-respect and inquiry appear both in and out of school. So, why not involve others in assisting in measurement of learning? To extend measurement to many more dimensions of student performance requires the development of a significantly larger number of instruments than are used today. It will also require far more record keeping. At the same time the efforts will be amply rewarded through the positive results of reliable and valid data made available to students and parents.

There is, however, a more basic concern about specific objectives in the current formulation of accountability. It is the requirement that objectives be stated in behavioral terms in order to assign responsibility for learning to the teacher. The use of objectives stated in behavioral terms limits the options to a single theory of learning, to the exclusion of other equally viable theories.

Behaviorism as a theory is an explanation of how and why man acts. It concentrates on the observable manifestations of stimulus and response. Man is viewed as a product of forces external to him. The control of external variables in proper order and intensity results in predictable behavior. There is no recognition of significant variables within the learners. Behaviorism is based on empiricism, with its emphasis on those factors which can be observed, controlled and quantified. It is on this view of learning that behavioral objectives rest.

Learning is defined differently in the Gestalt or cognitive-field division of psychology. Rather than through a conditioned response to a stimulus, learning takes place through insight or the reorganization of the perceptual field of the learner. There are internal factors within the learner which account for learning. The learner behaves in relation to his view of the environment. These internal factors are not amenable to the controls that behaviorists exert over environmental factors to produce learning. The learner is freed from the environmental constraints. Learning is more difficult to assess from this view because it does admit consideration of factors such as perception, emotion and feeling.

These admittedly brief descriptions of two major theories of the psychology of learning do bring out the pertinent point for accountability. The current formulation of accountability is based upon a theory of learning which holds that the learner has no control over the learning situation if the teacher arranges the proper stimuli in the needed order and intensity.

The teacher, then, is in absolute control of the learning situation. It follows that the teacher then can be held fully accountable for what the student learns. On the other hand there is another equally valid theory of learning which holds that the learner is not affected significantly by external variables, that learning takes place mainly within the learner. The learner's perception, feeling and emotion are the major influences on what is learned. The teacher, then, would not have significant control of the learning situation nor could be held fully accountable for what the student learns. The writer's bias is that teacher and student are equally accountable for what is learned in the classroom, but with others also having some accountability, for example parents, peers and the school administration. This will be discussed in another section.

The final part of this section deals with evaluation. A widely acceptable definition of evaluation is: the collection of reliable and valid information to assess whatever is being measured, and communicating the results to those who commissioned that evaluation. In some instances the report of the evaluation reaches still other audiences, usually through the public media.

The report of the evaluation is used in decision-making related to a particular program or project or in choosing options from alternatives. Hence, prior to the beginning of the evaluation the decision-makers need to meet with the evaluators to clearly state (1) what kinds of decisions are to be made and (2) what must be considered in making those decisions.

There are a variety of approaches to evaluation. Each approach usually includes the following stages:

(1)   Agreement by the sponsors and the evaluators on the nature of what is to be evaluated and the decisions that need to be made.

(2)   Design of the evaluation, e.g. what and who is to be measured and when.

(3)   Collection and analysis of data.

(4)   Reporting of the summary data.

Around the issue of accountability there are several problems related to evaluation. First, because evaluation is accomplished in order to make important decisions it is paramount to consider who should be involved in making those decisions. Frequently decisions are made by those far removed from the program or project that is to be evaluated. If one is to be held accountable it seems reasonable that the person should definitely be involved in determining what decisions need to be made as well as what needs to be considered in making those decisions. Even more obnoxious to those held accountable is the decision to have a program evaluated after it has been initiated.

Second, it seems promising that more use might be made of "goal free" evaluation. For this mode the evaluator is not told of the stated goals (outcomes) for a particular program or project; the evaluator looks for actual effects rather than checking on alleged effects. The evaluation is uncontaminated by statements of outcomes expected. This mode may be especially helpful in identifying appropriate outcomes of learning in aspects of education for which we have no adequate measures at the present time, such as in the aesthetics and affective areas, and in critical thinking.

Third, professionals in the field of measurement need to cooperate with others (lay as well as professional) to develop valid and reliable measures of the broad range of outcomes that the various publics in society expect of education and for which we have no instruments. The range of specific objectives in other than cognitive areas of education are numerous, and they should not be ignored because of current lack of measurability. Their measurement could begin through use of less refined techniques suoh as observations, proxies, and indicators. The point related to accountability is that both lay and professional people need to engage in the development of measures for assessing objectives of learning in the full range of dimensions considered to be important, rather than limiting measurement to exclusively cognitive areas for which current instruments exist.

Last, it is from the decisions that are made as a result of the summative evaluation that the "valuing" arises out of evaluation. It follows that if those to be held accountable need to be involved in determining what decisions should result from evaluation, they should also be involved in making the final decisions about that program or project. If accountability is to be a blessing, then those involved in the program need to have input into the valuing that results from evaluation.

In the current formulation of accountability there is a tendency to restrict the identification of specific learning objectives solely to those that can be measured, usually through existing tests, in basic skills of reading and mathematics. This tendency denies the existence of other dimensions of education that are of importance to the many publics that make up our society.

Professional educators (especially persons in the field of measurement) and lay people need to cooperate in the development of measures for all the dimensions of education that are important to various publics. Such instruments should include data noted from out-of-school behavior and performance as well as that exhibited in school. This would involve parents and others in the task of identifying evidence of learning.

One of the major concerns around the current formulation of accountability is its view of a single theory of learning described as behaviorism. It holds that only behavior which can be observed and quantified exists. External variables in proper order and intensity result in predictable behavior. The teacher, then, is in absolute control and can be held fully accountable for learning. However, there are other equally acceptable theories of learning which should be recognized and used in formulation of a concept of accountability. One example is the Gestalt or cognitive-field theory of learning that states that internal factors within the learner account for what is learned. It is the learner's insight, perception, emotion and feeling which most influence what is learned. In this case the teacher would have little control over what is learned; the student is far more liable and accountable.

It seems that blaming or ascribing accountability for learning to a single person is a prime impediment to developing a viable and workable formulation of accountability. There are direct and indirect impacts on both the teacher and the learner which must be considered in attempting to assign that for which each should be held accountable.

Finally, evaluation related to accountability is a crucial aspect of an accountability system that would be acceptable to both the general public and the profession. Both professionals and the public need to be involved in deciding what decisions are to be made as well as what should be considered in making those decisions. It is the "valuing" from evaluation that relates directly to the goals of education on which both the public and the professionals must collaborate.

The basic question inherent in the concept of accountability revolves around who has control of what, because one can be held accountable only for what he has control over. Control over the many variables of *human* learning definitely seems to exist in more than a single person— the learner, or in just two persons—the learner and the teacher. Take for example, a high school student who failed to learn anything in school on the day after he had a serious argument with his sweetheart because what went on in school was unimportant to him on that day. His sweetheart and their problem were in control. Or, the teacher who lost control of a learning situation because he did not have the needed range of instructional materials for the students in that class. The school administration was accountable for not providing the materials the students needed. Those two situations are fairly simple illustrations of the control of learning existing in other than the teacher or the student.

The two simple illustrations just related can easily be used to trace a chain of accountability both directly and indirectly. Numerous studies report the strong influence of peers on one's attitudes about what should or should not be learned and on one's motivations to learn, as well as expectations about education. Parents and siblings exert much influence on behaviors and attitudes about learning through the activities, practices and expectations that exist at home. Peers and the home situation directly affect the student and thereby remove his absolute control of some variables in the learning situations.

Similarly, there are factors reducing the absolute control of the teacher over some variables in the learning situations. Regardless of how one pictures the role of the teacher there seem to be these basic responsibilities of the person in that role: (1) diagnosing the current needs and gaps in what needs to be learned; (2) correctly prescribing the content, skills and processes to enable learning; (3) assessing what actually has or has not been learned, then repeating the cycle for further learning; and (4) accomplishing these responsibilities in a humane manner.

For those students who still, for whatever reasons, seem unable to learn the teacher has the responsibility of referral to appropriate sources for further diagnosis. To expect any teacher to be successful with each and every student is grossly unfair. No physician or lawyer is successful with one hundred percent of his patients or clients. The teacher is not in control if the school administration fails to provide the materials and help needed for diagnosis, the instructional aids and materials in the content and processes, and the instruments needed for assessment. The school administration is responsible for providing those elements. Likewise, the school administration is responsible for providing resources for further diagnosis of students who do not learn through the usual procedures and content. The major point is that persons, things or effects not in the classroom with the teacher and student may have direct influence on the learning situation.

An extension of what the teacher does or does not control can proceed from the school administration to what may be the responsibilities of the school board and the factors under its control. In previous sections of this essay it has been indicated that the school board has principal responsibility for establishing the forum through which goals for education acceptable to all the publics in a community may be stated. Those goals then serve as a base for the development of specific objectives of learning in classrooms. The board has responsibilty for setting policies in line with stated goals. It is responsible for funding the necessary materials, procedures and processes for attaining those goals. And it is responsible for making decisions based on the continual assessment and evaluation of the results of learning. All these responsibilities eventually have impact, positive or negative, on learning that occurs in classrooms.

A further extension of teacher control of factors can proceed to responsibilities of the state legislature. It is the legislature which makes all laws and regulations for education in the states. If its laws favor particular interests or views about the purposes of education then it exercises control and is accountable for certain factors in education. Its allocation of funds for education can result in absolute control over some factors. Its very political nature can strongly influence still other factors. The influence and authority of the state legislature and its relationship to the concept of accountability needs intensive study.

Similar extensions of the impact of others on the control of factors that influence learning may proceed from the student in a classroom situation. Beyond the family and home the student's learning is influenced by what he sees and experiences out in the community where he spends the greater portion of his waking hours. Younger and older persons in the community greatly influence his attitudes and behaviors about learning and other aspects of life. Persons in various institutions (religious, public and private) that he frequents have some impact on the student. Numerous studies speak to the influence on students of the public media, particularly TV, through which they experience immediately the social, political and other events that occur in the society and throughout the world. Even further, they experience the particular values and views depicted by the fictitious programs that are prolific during prime time TV and at other hours.

It should be clear to the reader that the stipulations of indirect influence which have been cited are empirically derived. The need for more precisely determining who has what degree of control over the many factors of learning in the chain of accountability is self-evident.

With all of the foregoing background about problems in implementing the concept of accountability, we proceed next to examine a just formulation of accountability.

Toward a Just Formulation of Accountability

The discussion of a just formulation of accountability will be limited to the viewpoints of citizens and teachers.

There is just concern of the citizens of this country about the increasing costs of education. With almost 50 million students and nearly 2 million teachers in schools, over 30 billion dollars in tax funds are spent to finance this huge enterprise. These costs have nearly doubled over the past decade. Citizens should not view accountability, however it is formulated, as a means of reducing the costs of education. For some years now all government agencies have operated under some accountability management procedures, but none has significantly reduced costs except through a reduction of services rendered. The cost of nearly every service utilized has at least doubled over the past decade, and those services have also frequently been reduced from what was formerly rendered. Much of the increase is due to inflation which is universal. So, one should be cautious and skeptical if promises of money savings are given because of the adoption of an accountability system.

Citizens also need to examine another premise that supports the current formulation of accountability. It has to do with the results, the products of a business or industry and the rendering of services provided by public institutions like education or private practitioners such as physicians. The product of business or industry is complete and finished when it is produced. The buyer uses it as is. On the other hand, the recipient of a service such as education or medicine has to internalize some elements of that service before he can benefit from them. The premise to be examined is: might we explore the need for different management concepts for practitioners in institutions that render services and assist recipients in getting the most benefit from those services? Unlike business and industry, there is an added dimension of interacting with human beings to get benefit of services. We might reduce confusion and clarify our expectations if we developed a service management concept to apply where it seems more appropriate than a business management application. This proposal in no way precludes the application of appropriate business *procedures* (such as accounting) to the operation of service institutions. It is the total system of managing the service of education that needs re-evaluation.

One other matter of fairness to be considered is: why should schools be singled out for a degree of accountability that is not demanded of other government institutions or of businesses and industries? Government other than education expends far more tax funds than does education. Every one is a consumer of the myriad of products from business and industry. For the sake of equity should not citizens demand the same degree of accountability for all public and private institutions, businesses and industries?

Another major concern of citizens is the inability of the education-profession to better demonstrate its effects on the learning of students. Citizens have a right to all the information about the status of learning in all schools. In public education all that occurs should be open to public scrutiny. This in no way means that there has to be an adversary relationship between the public and the profession. It does mean that the public must more clearly state its goals for education to the profession and the profession must be able and willing to seek to achieve the objectives that derive from those goals.

In sum, a just and fair formulation of accountability from the viewpoint of citizens would include:

(1)   An understanding that an accountability system is a tool for measuring effectiveness rather than a way of reducing costs.

(2)   A recognition of the significant differences in the operation of a business or industry and that of a service such as educaton, and that different management systems may be appropriate for each.

(3)   The application of the same degree of accountability should be extended to all firms and institutions, public and private.

(4)   An agreement of goals for education in every local school district.

For Teachers

Evidently there has to be a scapegoat for education in our society. Only a few years ago that scapegoat was the student. It was claimed that he alone was accountable for what was learned. If he failed to learn he was labeled slow, retarded or unmotivated. The schools were geared to deal with the majority who were already successful and to eject the one third who were difficult to educate. Many in the teaching profession promoted the idea of the student as the scapegoat.

With the advent of accountability a few years ago a new scapegoat has come to the fore. It is now the teacher. There are claims that the teacher alone is accountable for what the student learns. Teachers don't want to be the scapegoat any more than did students. It borders on the absurd to label any single individual, be it student or teacher, a scapegoat for the complex phenomenon of learning. In earlier sections of this essay attention was drawn to the fact that accountability for learning is jointly held by several persons directly and by still others indirectly. Hence, any just formulation of accountability will include the principle of shared responsibilty.

In the preceding section it was indicated that citizens need to state goals for education in that community. Only when there are definite goal statements may teachers be fairly charged with responsibility for certain results. Members of the teaching profession may then apply their specialized expertise to specific objectives derived from stated goals and be responsible for reasonable achievement of those objectives. They also have the obligation, in public education, of informing citizens of the results of what has or has not been accomplished. There needs to be no fear of appraisal of this nature, when citizens and professionals together attack the problems indicated.

The great majority of teachers, over three-fourths, support the principle of accountability. This is documented in several surveys made both by the teaching profession itself and by others. Teachers' feelings about implementing the principle is another matter. Their major concerns are about what is to be measured and what decisions are to be made as a result of evaluation. Each of these factors has been discussed in foregoing sections. The major consideration around these concerns is that teachers need to be involved in the decisions about these two factors.

Finally, there is an element of accountability on the part of individual teachers. The writer believes every teacher, or individual expecting to enter the teaching profession, is responsible for diligently demonstrating attitudes which reflect: (1) faith in the possibility of improving the human condition, (2) belief that all students can learn, so that there is a never-ending quest for facilitating learning, (3) expectation that those affected by a decision should be involved in making that decision and (4) willingness to accept fair appraisal.

From the viewpoint of teachers, then, a just formulation of accountability would include:

(1) Recognition that there is joint accountability for student learning and neither the student nor the teacher alone is solely accountable.

(2) Objectives derived from goals stated by the citizens of a local school district are the basis for informing citizens about the results of education.

(3) Provision for teachers to share in decisions about what is to be measured and what use is to be made of the results of evaluation.

Blessing or Affliction?

The concept of accountability is here to stay. This being the case it seems imperative to develop, as soon as possible, a formulation of accountability that will be fair and just for the many persons who unquestionably share some responsibility for what a student learns. To claim that only one individual is solely accountable for learning ingnores all evidence to the contrary and imposes a terrible burden on education in our society. On the other hand, a fair and just formulation including elements presented in this essay and others similar to these will be a blessing to education and to the students, teachers, parents, administrators, school boards and legislatures that jointly share accountability for the learning that occurs in our schools.

REFERENCES

Alkin, Marvin C. and Fitz-Gibbon, Carol T. "Methods and Theories of Evaluating Programs." *Journal of Research and Development in Education,* Vol. 8, No. 3, Spring 1975.

Bain, Helen. "Self Governance Must Come First, Then Accountability." *Phi Delta Kappan,* Vol. 51, No. 8, April 1970.

Bundy, Robert F. "Accountability: A New Disneyland Fantasy." *Phi Deltan Kappan,* Vol. 56, No. 3, November 1974.

Dobbs, Ralph C. "Accountability in the Learning Process." *Kappa Delta Pi Record,* Vol. 9, No. 4, April 1973.

Good, Thomas L., *et al.* "How Teachers View Accountability." *Phi Delta Kappan,* Vol. 56, No. 5, January 1975.

Harrison, Jr., Alton. "Teacher Accountability—A Fallacious Premise." *Kappa Delta Pi Record,* Vol. 9, No. 3, February 1973.

Hottleman, Girard D. "The Accountability Movement." *The Massachusetts Teacher,* Vol. 53, January 1974.

Leight, Robert L. *Philosophers Speak on Accountability in Education* (Danville, Ill.: The Interstate Printers and Publishers, Inc., 1973).

Olson, Arthur V. and Richardson, Joe A. *Accountability: Curricular Applications* Scranton, Pa.: Intext Educational Publishers, 1972.

Ovard, Glen F. "Teacher Effectiveness and Accountability."*NAASP Bulletin,* Vol. 59, No. 387, January 1975.

Sciara, Frank J. and Jantz, Richard K. *Accountability in American Education* Boston: Allyn and Bacon, Inc., 1972.

Taggart, Robert J. "Accountability and the American Dream." *The Educational Forum,* Vol. 39, No. 1, November 1974.

III.

TESTING: Its Use and Effect on Learners

By William F. Nolen
and Thomas J. Johnson

Although the laboratory of Wilhelm Wundt in Leipzig is usually considered the spawning ground of modern psychological and educational measurement and evaluation, testing and measurement have roots buried much deeper in antiquity. As early as the year 2200 B.C. the Chinese are said to have had an elaborate system of civil service examinations. Government appointments were awarded under this system on the basis of tested performance in the six arts: music, archery, horsemanship, writing, arithmetic and protocol.

Testing, however, was not restricted to the East. The ancient Greeks demonstrated considerable interest in both the theory and practice of mental and physical testing as measures of citizenship. The Greeks, as P.H. DuBois indicated about the Chinese, "recognized that relatively short performance under carefully controlled conditions could yield an estimate of the ability to perform under less rigorously controlled conditions and for a longer period of time." Vestiges of the Socratic tradition of instruction interspersed with oral examinations are still manifest in American education with our system of classroom recitation at the public school level and thesis orals in higher education.

Measurement and testing are far from new concepts, yet their uses have greatly expanded from employment as tools of selection in the Greek and Chinese cultures. It is appropriate that as our knowledge of human behavior continues to grow, the role of testing should be an expanded one. But this expansion should also be approached with caution.

Controversies surrounding the categorization or labeling of children and the evaluation of curricula often center on issues of testing. Many of these controversies involve legitimate criticisms of testing which are largely due to inappropriate utilization of tests.

Too many of the educational problems of our times are assessed with standardized tests, with the attitude that somehow standardization guarantees the appropriateness of the instrument. It should be emphasized that standardization of a test deals only with the "standardization" of the format of presentation and the rules of scoring of the instrument. It in no way assures the user of the appropriateness of the test for his purposes, or for comparison with any other equally "standardized" test.

Some who view testing as the ultimate decision point in a process fail to note the possible fallibility of the test. When tests are to be used as part of the decision process in an educational setting, the issue of fallibility should be considered from several points. First, is the test being used for the purpose for which it was designed? A standardized achievement test may reflect impressive figures concerning the test's reliability and validity. If, however, the test user employs this test, either explicitly or implicitly, as a measure of aptitude rather than achievement the results are questionable. Through the administration manual the test publisher has informed us that data are available which demonstrate that this particular test proved to be an accurate and valid measure of achievement (past learning) for some group on which the test was normed, for example, a national sample of fourth graders. If the user chooses to measure aptitude or scholastic potential with this test, he should be fully aware of the dangers of misinterpretation, and the need to gather empirical data relating performance on this test with future academic performance.

Secondly, fallibility may be due to the inaccuracy of the measurement qualities of the test itself. If the responses to specific stimuli (items) of a test are assigned numerical values by a process which is either not well defined or established on rules which are not theoretically supportable, results may reflect interpretations which are fallacious and detrimental to the learner.

The final issue concerning test fallibility is whether the behaviors sampled by particular test items reflect a satisfactory representation of the attribute which is under investigation. Behaviors that are sampled in any test may involve a constellation of traits so that the determination of one predominant trait is problematical. Measurement based on such behaviors may lead to a representation of the specific trait that reflects these other traits as well. This leads to varying interpretations, since we can never be sure just what is being measured.

This chapter will examine testing as it affects the learner. Evidence will be presented that clearly establishes the need for caution in the utilization and interpretation of tests in the educational decision process. The intent is not to kill the messenger because the message is bad, but rather to examine some of the reasons for the fallibility of the message itself. When these issues are considered, testing may be utilized as a valuable component of any learning system.

Testing as it is traditionally considered actually consists of three components: measurement, testing and evaluation. In order to better understand the possible use of tests, these three components will be briefly considered.

Measurement

Measurement involves the quantification of attributes or characteristics of persons, objects or events according to a specifically formulated set of ground rules. The physical measurement of attributes such as height or weight involve rules for assigning numbers that have been agreed upon and standardized to a point where everyone understands the procedures of assignment. This is an essential step if all observations of certain traits are to be quantified accurately and consistently.

Educational measurement also requires the quantification of characteristics or attributes under specified rules; however, the problem here is more complex. Measurement of attributes or characteristics must be inferred from measurements of behaviors on specific tasks. A student is spoken of as being of "average intelligence" when he performs at a certain level on specific tasks such as verbal reasoning or abstract reasoning. Since this is, in effect, one step removed from the attributes we wish to measure, the rules for quantification are less agreed upon than those in the realm of physical measurement. The cloudiness of these rules of number assignment to traits is often the beginning of our problems of accuracy and consistency of measures.

Testing

A test may be defined as any observation or series of systematic observations of task performance which are taken to represent some educational or psychological trait or attribute. When one thinks of tests, images of students responding to items or questions of an examiner are brought to mind. However, nothing in this definition suggests that tests can only be traditional paper-and-pencil measures of cognitive or intellectual attributes. In fact, many of the more interesting findings in educational or psychological research are systematically obtained while the subjects continue to function in their "natural" setting. What is important is that tests provide a series of task performance *stimuli* that are so controlled and sequenced that they yield systematic observations of the attribute in question.

When one thinks of tests, they are usually considered as being limited to multiple-choice, true-false, sentence completion or essay questions used to measure some level of performance in the cognitive domain. This conception of tests unnecessarily narrows the scope of behaviors which may be monitored. Students may be systematically observed in situations where the stimuli, although controlled and arranged, are not directly apparent. Such observations produce measures of behavior in settings that closely approximate reality. The value of these types of procedures becomes more obvious when we consider the following: the most valid measure of a behavior is the one which most closely approximates the behavior in question. For instance, an evaluation of a student's attitude toward school might be better achieved through classroom observation than by the use of a written attitude scale.

Evaluation

Tests should be designed to accurately measure the target attribute or characteristic. But no matter how reliable a test is, someone must interpret the results and decide upon program alternatives or alternate courses of action most suitable for the student. Evaluation then, is the process through which judgments and decisions are formulated from a wide variety of behaviors that have been sampled through systematic observations.

Before any important educational decisions are made, as much relevant information as possible about the student should be obtained. Great care should be exercised to insure that all behaviors from which we infer certain characteristics have been sampled. The person who forms decisions from an inadequate base of behaviors underlying the attribute in question is evaluating improperly. More important, he is subject to great risks regarding his prediction of the student's future behavior or the strength of the inferred attribute.

With these components of the testing process defined, the various test usages and test types will be examined with reference to learning systems.

Test Usage

Tests are administered with the hope that measurements from them will help in making appropriate decisions in different educational situations. While a test may be useful in one situation, it may be totally unsuitable for another. It is the responsibility of the test administrator to insure that the most appropriate test is used for a given purpose. Only when this care is exercised can we expect that the measures derived from tests will help in making better decisions. Tests help increase the effectiveness of decision making by increasing the amount of knowledge already known by the teacher. The use of tests as an aid in decision making presumes that these measurements can predict a more suitable course of action than would have been possible without the measures. If this is not the case, one must consider the costs in terms of both the tester and the subject as those which recover few benefits.

Tests as Screening Devices

Tests may be used to help decide whether a student will be accepted or rejected for admittance to a particular program or institution. Such tests must accurately discriminate between those who will succeed and those who will likely fail, and must do so with minimum risk to both the individual and the institution. There are basically two types of risk in this situation: admitting individuals who later fail or rejecting individuals who would have succeeded if admitted. An ideal screening test would predict perfectly; it would indicate a decision to accept only those who would prove successful, while rejecting all applicants who would have ultimately failed. Unfortunately, tests are fallible instruments and all selection decisions involve the risks described. The role of the test user is to minimize these risks as much as possible.

This may be partially accomplished by examining the empirical evidence presented by the designer or publisher of the instrument chosen. If we are asking a test to discriminate those who would be successful from those who would likely fail, the evidence presented should include the subsequent behavior of prior tested subjects in the particular program. Evidence that merely correlates scores on the test with ratings of people currently *in* the program should not be considered as evidence that the test is a good predictor of *success* in the program.

Selection decisions are greatly improved when the test items used for screening of applicants closely approximate the behaviors that will be required in the position. The closer the correspondence between the test tasks and the tasks required for success at the institution, the less risk the prediction will involve.

Tests of this type, while of little use in public schools other than in counseling situations, are commonly used to predict ability to do college level work. SAT's are an example of a screening test. Much empirical testing is required to develop tests capable of discriminating among individuals. This testing has to be frequently updated to insure the accuracy of the prediction.

Tests in Placement

Tests are also used as tools in placing students in programs which are best suited for their needs. This type of testing differs from a simple selection decision. It must yield more than criteria for an accept or reject decision. Placement examinations should yield profiles of student performance on multiple variables or traits. These profiles must be related to the features of the program options available. The confusion between tests used in selection and those used in placement leads to the nonfunctional labeling of children. If scores on a test are used to assign students to "tracks" on the basis of prior performance only, we should not delude ourselves by calling this a "placement" decision.

A test may be a useful predictive tool in selection but ineffective in proper program selection. For example, a test of general aptitude might be able to predict whether an individual will succeed at college or not, but the selection of the program most suited to his background and needs would require considerably more information about his other attributes. Proper consideration would involve a test that sampled a broader spectrum of behaviors. Again, the user's best assurance that the risks involved in a placement decision are reduced is to demand that test items represent behaviors applicable to the various program alternatives.

Tests in Diagnosis

A test that assesses a person's performance in terms of a detailed view of strengths and weaknesses in order to improve performance serves a diagnostic function. Such a test should not only point out potential failures, but also should suggest causes for the deficiencies and provide a guide for a program of remediation. The use of tests for placement and diagnosis may overlap. A student may be placed in a remedial group if diagnostic information indicates that this is the most suitable placement.

Diagnostic tests may be used to different degrees. Those that identify students who have problems are in the broadest sense called diagnostic. But this does not agree with the definition of diagnostic testing which includes the presentation of a detailed picture of strengths and weaknesses. This should not be surprising, for a test can only sample a limited number of tasks measuring potential sources of problems. Tests that simply identify and define attributes must be supplemented by more extensive testing. For example, the Differential Aptitude Test (DAT) consists of eight subtests that previous research indicates are relevant to certain types of educational and vocational performance. Subjects who score low on any one or several of these subtests may be identified as having some kind of problem. However, diagnosing the specific nature of the problem would necessitate the use of additional diagnostic testing due to the complex nature of the attributes being measured.

Ideally, diagnostic tests should be comprised of items that break down more complex behaviors into tasks that sample component subskills. The test user should be confident that the test being employed contains an adequate sample of items representative of the skill at the proper level of specificity and that the skills being sampled are as free as possible from other sources of difficulty. Again an example may be helpful. If a child were having a problem reading, an appropriate diagnostic test might contain samples of items which dealt with sight vocabulary, recognition of consonant blends, or reversal of letters. These tasks sould be free of other confounding factors such as a particular size and form of print that might be confusing to the student.

Many commercially available tests purport to be diagnostic. Again, diagnosis is a question of degree. Any test which discriminates successful students from nonsuccessful ones could claim to be diagnostic in the most general sense. But the components that make up a diagnostic test do not correspond with those that comprise a survey test and any test which professes to contain both should be held suspect. Survey tests are meant to discriminate levels of achievement across the total range of the group. This is not the focus of a diagnostic instrument. In fact, interest usually centers on the bottom 10 to 15 percent of test scores for a sample and discrimination across the group is irrelevant. Since our interests center on the lower portion of the group, this is where the accuracy of our measures should be emphasized. Estimates of reliability and error of measurement should be furnished for this portion of the sample. Unfortunately this is not generally the case with the publishers of diagnostic tests.

Tests as Feedback

Evidence suggests that feedback from tests increases student learning and decreases the error rate. Generally, the more specific and immediate the feedback, the greater the learning. This is demonstrated not only by direct measures of student performance but also in the student's feeling concerning this use of tests.

In one study college students were asked to complete a questionnaire on the effects of weekly quizzes on achievement and attitude. Eighty percent said that the quizzes helped them learn more. It was also learned that when such tests were used as feedback, only 2 percent of the students responded that the quizzes created anxiety. The emphasis here is on the use of tests as learning tools, rather than as a means of punishing students who fail to live up to teacher or parental expectations. Sometimes students are able to locate their own errors and provide their own feedback; more often the teacher acts as facilitator in this process.

Tests may be constructed to provide two kinds of feedback. First the student's performance may be compared with the average performance of some specified reference group (other members of the class or a national sample of peers). When tests are used to compare an individual with others, they are called *norm-referenced tests*. Norm-referenced tests indicate that a particular student has more or less of the attribute in question than do other members of the reference group. If a test is so easy or so hard that performance is relatively non-varying it will not be very useful in assessing the individual's place among his peers. A norm-referenced test should be constructed so as to maximize the differences among individuals.

The second kind of feedback emerges when the student's performance is compared with some established criteria for example, spelling seven of ten words correctly. This type of test is referred to as a *criterion-referenced test.* In contrast to norm-referenced tests, criterion-referenced tests compare the student not with reference to other students but in relationship to some expected level of performance. The student may be required to attain some level of mastery before he is allowed to proceed to more complex learning levels. The advantages of criterion-referenced tests as a means of feedback over norm-referenced tests lie in the level of specificity and immediacy of feedback. The student may receive feedback regarding his place in class for a certain examination, but this use of the test as a pedagogical technique leaves much to be desired. This kind of feedback does not specify the areas of error for the student, but only his place among his peers. Criterion-referenced tests deal with specific task performance and offer the student more immediate and specific feedback of his performance. If feedback from tests is to be used as a learning tool it must involve more than giving the student a rank on the performance sampled.

As stated earlier, the intent of norm-referenced tests is to maximize individual differences. This is not the desired effect of criterion-referenced tests, since it is hoped that in time every student will reach the specified level of performance. Similar care must be exercised to insure that the sample of items used do, in fact, determine the subject's ability to achieve certain levels of performance. Just as norm-referenced tests that demonstrate little ability to discriminate are virtually useless, so too are items that do not accurately predict successful performance on the skill being tested.

Tests as Motivators

Tests used for diagnostic work and mastery can be used to motivate students to learn. Since students study for the type of examination they expect to take, it is the teacher's responsibility to construct examinations that reflect the objectives taught and measure significant educational outcomes. If examinations measure trivia, then students are encouraged to study trivia. When constructing a test, teachers should bear in mind that their goal is to assess significant educational outcomes; not to see if students have read the book or have been attentive in class. These latter points tend to generate trivial questions.

Examinations can affect students either positively or negatively. Students can perceive tests as threats or punishment and become fearful and anxious. If, however, tests have been emphasized as tools for diagnosis and mastery, the teacher can help students overcome needless anxieties related to the taking of tests.

Several conditions contribute to the use of examinations as motivators. Examinations should not be seen by the student as one-time indicators of success or failure. The use of one test as criteria for course completion has doubtful pedagogical value, and also creates for many students such a level of anxiety that performance is actually inhibited. Directions and test layout should encourage the best possible performance. In a study, in which three different sets of instructions were used for the same examination, students who received the more "ego-involving" directions performed significantly better. The test layout should group items logically and according to construction form. Again the goal of an examination is to assess significant learning outcomes, not to see how rapidly a student can "change gears" while covering the various content areas of the test.

In some cases it may be necessary at first to avoid written examinations as much as possible until students learn that tests can be of benefit to them. Students will be more willing to be examined if tests are taken in an atmosphere of trust and mutual benefit.

Tests in Curriculum and Program Evaluation

Tests may be used to make decisions about programs and curricula. In these cases, tests are used not to measure individual students' behavior but to assess the overall program and elements within it. *Program-referenced* testing requires that the test used as an index of the program's effectiveness maintains a maximum relationship with what was actually taught in the program. Thus for most program-evaluation purposes pupil performance on standardized achievement tests will not be an adequate indicator of how well a given program worked. Unfortunately, school districts tend to rely on standardized tests to assess the effectiveness of their programs, while the evidence shows that these tests are inappropriate for this use.

Evaluations of this type also permit cost benefit decisions. Every new program involves costs, from books to buildings. Tests may be used to assess whether the benefits are worth these costs. Tests can also be used to evaluate new programs by comparing outcomes with unintended consequences. If, for example, a new curriculum raises achievement level but lowers attitudes, a program change may warrant consideration.

Tests in Theory Development

Many educational and psychological theories have developed from the systematic observation of subjects performing tasks under controlled conditions. Piaget's theory of cognitive development, for example, is based on this type of clinical observation. As we continue to develop means of assessment that more closely relate to specific tasks, further theories to explain these behaviors will evolve.

Testing has also contributed a substantial theory of its own, that of *psychometrics*. This science is committed to a better understanding of principles of measurement. It seeks to provide a clearer picture of relationships among different factors and variables. New technologies and areas of assessment are forthcoming that will contribute to theories of personality, intelligence, attitudes, and other hypothetical constructs.

Test Types

Tests may be classified in the following way: (a) under the conditions they are administered (individual or group tests); (b) by the methodology of scoring (objective or subjective); (c) by the response mode (performance or paper-and-pencil tests); and, (d) by the degree of standardization (teacher-made or commercially published tests).

Individual and Group Tests

Tests administered to one person at a time are *individual* tests; those given to many persons at one time are *group* tests. Most individually administered tests are given orally and demand the constant attention of a trained examiner. The examiner is concerned not only with the subject's responses, but also with the manner of response. This kind of observation requires special training and experience. Only examiners with appropriate background should consider administering an individual test. The American Psychological Association issues guidelines that indicate the required training for various types of testing. Individual tests are usually administered by school psychologists or counselors who are trained to elicit the most typical performance from a student and to accurately observe and record how the student responds. Students can profit from freedom in responding to certain tasks; however, this freedom is constrained by the standardization of procedures dictated by various individual tests. One solution would record responses given within the frame of standardization such as a time limit. The examiner would then allow the subject to continue working on the task in order to both motivate the subject and get a better picture of how the subject deals with various problems.

Because individual tests are time consuming to administer and require special skills, they are usually used only when crucial decisions are necessary. In typical classroom situations group tests are adequate for measuring cognitive skills. While group tests require little training to administer, their interpretation may be far from simple. Both individual and group test interpretation require a great deal of skill and knowledge. We have also seen that group tests require considerable skill in accurately measuring the sampled behaviors, as well as insight by the user regarding the test's appropriateness for the particular purpose.

Objective and Subjective Tests

Objectivity of a test refers only to the scoring procedure and not to item content. Tests are objectively scored when observers agree on how responses should be scored. Test items are said to be objectively scored when the "rules" governing the assignments of weights to responses are so well defined that observers will always agree. These procedures have been so well delineated on many tests that scoring can be accomplished through computer processing.

Subjective tests allow the scorer considerable latitude in determining the appropriateness of subjects' responses, an approach not specified by the principles of measurement. But there is no guarantee that an objectively scored test is representative of the behavior that the user wishes to sample; nor is a subjectively scored test necessarily a poor indicator of that same behavior.

Performance and Paper-and-Pencil Tests

Performance tests are nonverbal examinations that require a subject to perform a specific task under certain control conditions. These tests are usually administered individually so that the examiner may carefully monitor the behavior of the subject as each task is attempted. Many individually administered intelligence tests yield a verbal and performance score. Discrepancies between these two types of scores often indicate a need for further testing. Types of performance tests differ considerably from picture arrangement and picture completion tasks to dexterity measures. Their common feature is the measure of a subject's ability to perform certain tasks, rather than respond to questions.

Paper-and-pencil tests are usually given in group situations. Subjects are asked to record responses to questions on an answer sheet. This procedure allows the examiner to test large groups of people at one time. These tests may be verbal or nonverbal, depending on the mode of presentation. Careful analysis of results of these tests may yield much valuable information, and, in fact, when one considers the constraints of the classroom they are probably the most efficient manner of sampling students' behavior.

Teacher-Made and Commercially Published Tests

Teacher-made tests are those constructed by the classroom teacher. They are dependent upon the teacher's skill in measurement and evaluation. Commercially published tests are constructed by experts in the content area. Both of these tests may be "standardized", in terms of instruction format, and "normed" on some sample of the students' peers, although this is more often limited to commercially published tests. Commercial tests include larger and more broadly defined norming samples than tests designed by a teacher or a school system. But this does not mean that the commercial instrument is an inherently better measure of student performance when compared with a teacher-made test. The teacher-made test may lack the extensive norming procedures of the publisher's test, but it may possess properties which allow for a more appropriate assessment of target behaviors. For example, it was noted earlier that program-referenced testing would demand the "tailor-made" quality of a teacher-made or school-made test in order to map to the objectives of the program in question. It must be emphasized that a test is only valuable when it samples performance from behaviors of interest to the user.

Conclusion

The focus of this chapter has been on the various uses and types of tests as they affect the learner in educational settings. While many technical concepts such as reliability, validity, item difficulty and item discrimination have been only indirectly addressed, these concepts are discussed fully in books dealing with testing and measurement. Many times the test user finds himself caught up in a spiral of technical information and common misconceptions to such a degree that the required relationship between the rationale underlying the test and the purpose of the testing is lost. If we, as test users, constantly press for significant educational outcomes, we will demand much more rigor from our testing techniques. If our intent is to use tests as instructional management tools, we must demand from them evidence of the highest quality since our decisions based on them do have consequences for people involved. Finally, as takers of tests, we must demand that when they are used as tools for decision making about us, that they are of high enough quality for us to accept the personal consequences of decisions made through them.

REFERENCES

Cronbach, L. J. *Essentials of Psychological Testing,* 3rd. Edition, New York: Harper and Row Publishers, Inc., 1970.

Cronbach, L.J., Gleser, G. C., Nanda, H., and Rajaratnam, N. *The Dependability of Behavioral Measurements.* New York: Wiley, 1970.

Dubois, P. H. *A History of Psychological Testing.* Boston: Allyn and Bacon, Inc., 1970.

"A Test Dominated Society: China 1115 B.C.-1905 A.D." J. J. Barnette (Ed.), *Readings in Psychological Tests and Measurement,* (Rev. Ed.), Homewood, Illinois: Dorsey, 1968.

Feldhusen, J. F. "Student Perceptions of Frequent Quizzes and Postmortem Discussions of Tests." *Journal of Educational Measurement,* 1, No. 1, June 1964.

Stanley, J. C. and Hopkins, K. D. *Educational and Psychological Measurement and Evaluation,* 5th Edition, Englewood Cliffs: Prentice-Hall.

Thorndike, R. L. and Hagen, E. P. *Measurement and Evaluation in Psychology and Education,* 3rd Edition, New York: John Wiley and Sons, Inc., 1969.

Yamamoto, K. and Kizney, H. F. "Effects of Three Sets of Test Instruction on Scores on an Intelligence Test." *Educational and Psychological Measurement,* 25, No. 1, 1965.

IV.

CONTINUING EDUCATION AND HOW IT RELATES TO A LIFE LONG PROCESS

By Stanley M. Grabowski

Our educational perspective must change if we are to accommodate ourselves to a rapidly changing society. As recently as a generation ago, one could repeat the old story about the professor who brought the examination questions to the printer. After looking over the set of questions the printer said, "These are the same questions as last year." And the professor defended them by saying, "Yes, the questions are the same, but the answers are different this year."

We are living at a time when not only the answers are different, but the questions are changing as well. Sweeping and radical changes have taken place in many areas of life. Economic, political, social, and philosophical systems have been marked by changes in industrialization, automation, population growth, and decolonization. These changes continue and will extend far into the future. Margaret Mead has said that none of us will ever die again in the world in which we were born.

The rapidity of change is staggering. It is occurring faster than we expect. For example, at the New York World's Fair in 1939, just as

World War II was beginning, the "World of Tomorrow" was the theme of the fair. It depicted what we might expect around the year 2000. Needless to say we have far surpassed what was predicted back in 1939.

The progress the human race is making is evidenced in the shortening of eras or epochs in history. The Stone Age lasted about 500,000 years; the Iron Age extended over some 5000 years; the Bronze Age covered nearly 5000 years; the Industrial Age accounted for about 500 years; the Atomic Age has been with us for only 50 years; the Space Age is just about 10 years old; and we are now in the Computer Age. How long will it last before some other phenomenon replaces it? Peter Drucker calls the present period the "Age of Discontinuity"; meaning that unless one continues to learn, one becomes obsolete. What youths have learned by the time they leave the formal system of education around age 21 and what makes them productive at that age will not serve them by the time they have lived to be 40.

There was a time when formal education was supposed to serve as a permanent preparation for one's entire work life. Whatever one learned during the years of formal schooling would be sufficient to see one through in a chosen occupation until retirement. That situation has changed drastically. Even so-called blue collar workers are now required to relearn their jobs or learn new jobs anywhere from three to five times during their work life.

Not only blue collar workers, but professional people are also faced with obsolescence. In the case of professionals, educators speak about the "half-life" of a professional's competence. "Half-life" represents the time after completion of professional training when one becomes about one-half as competent as one was upon completion of training. One psychologist has figured out that the average half-life of professionals runs anywhere from five to twelve years, varying from one profession to another. The reason for this half-life competence is two-fold: first, an individual tends to forget some of the things learned in the process of preparatory training; second, new knowledge and developments go on while the professional is busy practicing. The difference between what one has forgotten and the new developments is the obsolescence gap—the area the professional must learn and relearn in order to stay abreast of the profession.

Dorothy Hutchinson neatly summarizes the professional's plight in this way:

> Obsolescence is the loss of acquired knowledge and the non-acquisition and/or non-utilization of new knowledge. It cannot be dismissed as mere stupidity, inability, or stagnancy. To be sure, some find obsolescence a tolerable condition. For many others it is a threat of terrifying proportions. Many practitioners identify with Lewis Carroll's Red Queen: "It takes a lot of running to stay in the same place."

Worker obsolescence is brought about by progress. As new technologies are invented, old jobs are replaced by newer ones, often creating several jobs to replace one old job. The rapidity of increase in new jobs can be quickly gleaned from the *Dictionary of Occupational Titles* which shows that the number of job titles has almost doubled in the last generation.

Some people make the mistake of viewing people in terms of obsolescence rather than looking at their jobs as being obsolescent. This mentality led Peter Drucker, at the 1975 annual conference of the American Society for Training and Development, to comment: "This talk about 'burned out' people is mostly nonsense! What people need most is 'repotting' and it perhaps is the greatest need in a society of organizations."

Most para-professionals, skilled workers, and professionals are forced to continue their education in order to stay on top of their jobs and fields of interest. Many other individuals must also continue their education. John Ohliger compiled a vast bibliography dealing with the various kinds of continuing education individuals are obliged to pursue. He concluded that we now have "compulsory adult education." Ohliger is referring to mandatory continuing education, some of which is imposed by law upon some groups who are subject to re-licenture as well as upon those who are professionally pressured into continuing education. He catalogued a partial list of the groups subject to compulsory adult education:

> Traffic offenders and judges; parents of delinquents and public school teachers; illiterates on welfare; nurses; pharmacists; physicians; optometrists; nursing home administrators; firemen; policemen; dentists; psychiatrists; dieticians; podiatrists; preachers; veterinarians; many municipal, state, provincial, and federal civil servants; employees of all types pressured into taking courses, classes, or joining sensitivity training or organizational development groups; and, of course, the military, where most, if not all adult education is compulsory (Ohliger, 1974).

In addition to mandatory adult education, there are increasing numbers of adults pursuing voluntarily some form of education. The figures for adult participation in education vary from a conservative 25 million to a generous 60 million, depending upon who is counting and what criteria are used to determine participation. It appears that we have reached a point where more adults are engaged in education than young people, at all levels of the formal system of education.

All predictions for the future based on demographic data and population growth rates indicate that our nation is fast becoming filled with adults rather than children. Already there are about 45 million adults 55 years and over, and half of these are past age 65. As more elementary and secondary schools close down because there are not enough students to fill them, continuing education programs are expanding. We are an older population retiring earlier, as early as 53 years of age in some industries, and living longer. With shorter work weeks, longer vacations, and earlier retirement, most American adults have more leisure than any other previous generation. Many adults are turning to educational activities to use up some of the increased leisure time.

Definition of Terms

Anyone who reads the literature pertaining to the education of adults discovers that many labels are used to describe it. For example, some of the terms used include the following: adult education continuing education, continuous learning, lifelong learning, lifelong education, recurrent education, discontinuous education, *l'education permanente,* and career education.

One of the problems educators encounter in trying to find a satisfactory label for the education of adults is the lack of a common understanding and agreement as to the scope and content of the field. The field covers a wide range of activities including literacy and fundamental education; vocational and job training; political and civic education; religious education; economic education; social education; education about health; career and family problems; physical and personal development; education for self-fulfillment; and community development.

In addition there are various methods and techniques of learning used in the education of adults. Some of these include self-learning, independent study, group discussions, workshops, regular classes and lectures, on-the-job training, radio and television educational programs, night school classes, residential conferences and meetings, and correspondence study.

All definitions are dangerous, because they can obstruct and confuse as well as define. But it may be useful to look briefly at three of the most widely used terms in the education of adults: adult education, continuing education, and career education. All three terms deal with education. This is important to note because all of them refer to systematic learning, organized and planned to produce specific results; such as changes in knowledge, skills, attitudes and behavior. In this sense education differs from the kind of learning which takes place as a result of spontaneous interaction with our environment. Coolie Verner calls the first kind "Learning by design," and the latter "Learning by chance." Put another way, we *may* learn from experiences, but we do not engage in the random experiences in order to learn. All education involves learning; but all learning is not education.

Adult Education is the all-inclusive umbrella term, used to designate any "process by which the instructional needs of adults, as perceived by themselves or others, are met through organized learning experience." (Gideon, *et al.,* 1971). This definition includes any purposeful effort toward self-development carried on by an adult. Some people view adult education as exclusive of formal higher education and any education under direct legal compulsion. Others would restrict adult education to basic skills such as literacy. Perhaps the best use of the term *adult education* relates to the general meaning of *"education of adults;* the way an adult approaches learning.

Continuing Education is an unfolding process whereby an individual develops a learning program when basic formal education ends, and carries it on throughout a lifetime. It is a means of updating knowledge and skills in one's career, or can add new knowledge and skills in a different field. Continuing education embodies all forms of education including vocational, remedial, recreational, liberal, technical, professional, religious, and family life.

Continuing education is more than adult education if adult education is limited to "catching up" or "remedying" the gaps in one's earlier formal education. It is organized learning often directed towards a special competence. In this sense physicians, nurses, dentists, engineers, clergy, and teachers continue to study in order to stay informed of new developments in their fields. But continuing education is not for professionals only; it can serve any adult who wants to meet the educational needs of each successive period of life. It is open-ended with as many entry and exit points as a person needs.

Continuing education is linked to lifelong learning and is part of the total cycle, although it may be discontinuous. An individual may periodically return to further education, but do nothing in an active, formal way in between those experiences. Addressing this issue, Dorothy Hutchinson says that continuing education:

> tends to be sporadic, fragmented, nonsequential. It develops in response to crises. Its planning is shaped by expediencies. It is rife with duplication, deficits, and compartmentalization. Often in institutions of higher education educators preoccupied with undergraduate and graduate levels, relegate continuing education to the periphery. Yet the undergraduate curriculum should be considered the first orbit for continuing education (Hutchinson, 1973).

The method used for continuing education depends on the preference of the individual. It may consist of regular university courses, or self-directed reading, or attendance at conferences and meetings.

In a later chapter David Gardner will describe *career education* from several perspectives. From the perspective of adult education, career education is "the precess of helping a student to understand accurately both himself and the world of work, the specific educational and job requirements of occupations, entry and progress in educational pursuits, and, ultimately, the choice of a vocation" (Edington and Conley, 1973, p. 1). Career education is not confined to adults. It begins in grade one or earlier and continues through adulthood. Career education includes a combination of competence in the use of knowledge, a compassionate and empathetic appreciation of values, and a mastery of selected skills; all of which prepare a person for continued progress throughout life.

In a sense, career education is a sort of pre-service training which an individual can undertake repreatedly, as often as career changes occur. However, career education must not be thought of simply in terms of a job.

> The concept of career education is not based merely upon a need for new job skills but upon a recognition that for most of our children a meaningful and productive

work experience is essential to self-fulfillment. While the concept of lifelong learning recognizes the immediate need of many persons to upgrade their skills, it is also based on the recognition that learning can be a pleasure, a form of recreation (U.S. DHEW, 1972, pp. 3-4).

Everyone ought to be engaged in career education as a basis for other forms of education, but not restricted to it. We must be concerned with the development of the whole person in the broadest sense. This encompasses not only education for occupational, vocational, and professional competence, but also education for personal and family competence, for social and civic competence, and for self-realization. Beyond basic career education we must look to adult and continuing education to help develop the whole person. For this reason many educators are using the term "adult and continuing education" as an appropriate way to speak about the education of adults.

Continuing Education Options

Knowledge has often been equated with power. In our present society this seems to be increasingly the case. In our modern, technological society, education is a key source of that power. In this country, the formal education system has been the predominant source of knowledge power. In the last decade increasing numbers of individuals have been questioning whether this highly organized system can continue to meet contemporary societal needs.

The educational system casts education in terms of a sequential ladder of progression. The system was designed to move in linear progression from one level to another. An individual is programmed to move from the elementary grades through secondary school, and then into post-secondary schooling such as junior/community colleges, four year colleges and universities. Provision is made in the system for professional training on the graduate and even post-graduate levels. Theoretically, the product of this system of schooling is supposed to be an "educated person."

The truth is that we have countless individuals who possess certificates, diplomas, and degrees but who are "uneducated." The problem with our educational system is that it gives the impression that an individual is "finished" with learning once the individual has earned a diploma. Institutions as well as the people who pass through them have lost sight of the fact that graduation is really a commencement and that there is much to follow by way of more learning. Commencement must mean that there really is no such thing as an "educated person"; there are only people who are in the process of learning.

The idea of continuing education implies lifelong learning, but should not be made synonymous with lifelong schooling. Peter Drucker points out that over-extended schooling and continuing education are in opposition. Extended education operates on the premise that an individual ought to try to learn as much as possible before embarking upon an occupation or profession. Consequently, the longer an individual prolongs extended education, the more the individual will have learned. Continuing education, on the other hand, operates on the premise that certain things are learned best as an adult; that experience will not only provide the motivation to learn, but also will create a more capable learner.

The vast sociological changes which have come about since the end of World War II have dictated some radical changes in the old belief that preparatory schooling in the educational system is effective.

> [There] is an incipient recognition among adults who teach and administer in the core system of schools and colleges that they lack the prophetic and practical wisdom to judge how to prepare youth for a future society, some of whose characteristics will most likely exhibit significant discrepancies with the past. Social definitions of the responsibilities and tasks of adult roles are changing rapidly and will probably continue to do so. This is challenging our belief in the efficacy of a system of formal schooling of youth designed to prepare them for adulthood (U.S. DHEW, p. 52).

The old model of an educational system that starts with where the system is and where it wants to go must give way to a new model that starts with where the individuals are. Such a model looks to the needs of individuals, their aspirations, and their goals. A program is then developed that is a compromise between the goals of the individuals and the goals of the system into which the individuals are trying to integrate themselves.

Along with starting toward where the individuals want to go, the new system must provide individuals with alternatives from which they can choose. Individuals, if they are to develop fully as human beings, must have alternatives from which they can choose, even if their choices are wrong.

Another reason for providing alternatives to individuals was articulated by Stephen K. Bailey, Vice President for Governmental Relations of the American Council of Education, at the opening celebration of the Regional Learning Service of Central New York. In the belief that "Options in education will produce educative options," he suggested that *education* and *options* may well be the touchstones of the future. I place education first, because uneducated grabs at options is one manifestation of our current malaise. *Education* at its best results in a sophisticated understanding of the unhappy consequences of selecting options lightly: selecting mates lightly, selecting jobs lightly, selecting occupational and materialistic halters lightly, selecting avocation lightly. Education at its best is the creation of high standards for oneself and for society. It challenges people to aspire to those activities, skills, disciplines, and behaviors that bring lasting rewards--rewards in terms of ego satisfactions, rewards in terms of social amelioration and equity, rewards in terms of what Maslow has called 'self-actualization.'"

Recognizing the need to reform our present approach to education, the educators meeting at the Galaxy Conference on Adult Education in 1969 issued "Imperatives for Action." Among the suggestions and recommendations they made were the following:

> The American people desperately need an adequate system of life-long learning to enable us to remedy past deficiencies and to direct the forces of change toward humane ends. This lack cannot be filled merely by improving conventional schooling designed to prepare young people for the future, important as that may be. It must be filled by meeting continuous challenge with continuous response. Life-long learning must be made an all pervasive influence through which those who are responsible for today's critical decisions and choices—the adults of our nation—control the present and create the future we want.

> For the achievement of these goals, it is imperative that adult and continuing education be made a vital instrument of national purpose:

> To prepare each person to understand and cope with the issues of our time.

> To remedy educational deficiencies.

> To provide everyone with equal opportunity for meaningful work at decent pay—in preparation, access and advancement.

> To function more effectively as workers, parents, neighbors, citizens.

> To improve the quality of our lives—physical and spiritual, individual and social.

> To enable us to share meanings, values, purposes and power with ourselves and other peoples, in a world where constructive sharing is the only alternative to mutual destruction.

In line with these recommendations, the National Advisory Council on Extension and Continuing Education recommended in its Ninth Annual Report that Congress adopt the following declaration:

> To establish a policy of Lifelong Learning, Congress declares that it is in the national interest that opportunities for life-long learning through continuing education be available to all citizens without regard to previous education or training; and that consideration of sex, age, social and ethnic background, or economic circumstances shall not restrict access to all of such opportunities to any individual...

Continuing education must offer enough alternatives for individuals to extend educational opportunities over a lifetime. In such a configuration, continuing education provides individuals with greater opportunities to determine their future. This is especially true for those individuals for whom the traditional school system has failed: the force-outs (there really are no drop-outs) who will get new experiences outside the system.

All of us learn from sources other than formal instruction in the schools; we learn from our families, from our friends, from our associates, from our jobs, from our experiences, and from various other sources such as radio, television, and the print media. All of these can be used as part of one's continuing education, as can many other sources.

There are now many ways in which adults can continue their education, both inside and outside the formal system. Many new opportunities are following a non-traditional format even in the area of formal certification. Numerous college degree programs available to adults have started within the past ten years. For example, there are special degree programs leading to baccalaureate, masters and doctoral degrees which do not require attendance at classes on campus. In New York City there is a Master of Business Administration program offered to business executives on the commuter train between the suburbs and New York. Nova University in Florida offers a doctorate through a combination of independent studies and meetings with other students and "travelling professors." In New York State, college degrees in certain fields may be obtained by satisfactorily completing a series of examinations alone.

College credit can even be obtained by means of television courses and through newspapers.

Some colleges and universities are prepared to give college credit for life experiences, although the problem of how to translate life experiences into credit hours has been difficult to solve.

The list of non-traditional degree programs includes the following: Empire State College, Open College of Pennsylvania, Open University, University Without Walls, Regents External Degree Program, Independent Study Degree Program, Extended University.

Most of these non-traditional degree programs allow adults to pursue their education at their own pace without forcing them to complete a degree within a prescribed number of years. These programs acknowledge the fact that there are increasing numbers of individuals who are pursuing degrees on a part-time rather than a full-time basis.

In addition to degree programs adults have almost unlimited access to numerous educational opportunities that satisfy both societal and personal goals. A sample of these opportunities include the following: visits to museums, libraries, and botanical gardens; participation in political campaigns; attendance at religious services; attendance at various forms of cultural entertainment; participation in Cooperative Extension Services; participation in activities at the place of employment including business and industry, the military, government agencies at all levels; participation in programs sponsored by private organizations and associations; professional organizations; and the myriad of opportunities afforded by "proprietary" or business schools, television, and correspondence or home study courses.

Increasingly, adults are seeking education on their own. They are planning and directing their own study. Allen Tough's research found that the average individual undertakes about eight learning projects a year, spending around 700 hours a year altogether. Much of this learning is done by the individual without help from others.

Recent developments in educational and instructional technology have made available various teaching-learning programs such as audio cassettes, slides, programmed instruction books, and videotapes.

Along with the proliferation of new institutional forms for continuing education, a new concept has been developed for servicing the learning needs of individuals. Adult Education Resource Centers are coming into existence on the national, state, regional, and local levels. All of these centers try to meet the needs of the individual but with different emphases and with different services. On the national level, the Educational Resource Information Center (ERIC) operated by the National Institute of Education is a storage retrieval, and dissemination system providing ready access to documents in various areas of education. Current information relevant to education is listed in ERIC reference publications. Through these references any individual has easy access to a large store of information. Similar national systems are in operation covering other fields such as the sciences, technology, and health.

Continuing Education Model

The approach to continuing education dictates lifelong self-directed education with or without outside implementation. The approach places the major burden of continuing education planning upon the individual.

Most of the models for self-directed continuing education follow the same basic pattern. The model presented below is based on one originally proposed by Alan Knox in 1974. This model has five interrelated components: needs, setting, objectives, activities, and evaluation.

(1) Needs.   An individual must first identify the gaps between present behavior and desirable behavior. "Behavior" is used here to include knowledge, attitudes, skills, and any combination of these three.

The gaps are weaknesses or deficiencies an individual identifies in content, performance, goals, process, or opportunities. These gaps can be identified in one's professional competencies by comparison with the standards established by the profession. In other areas of continuing education an individual can more readily perceive gaps without outside standards of comparison.

(2) Setting.   Once the gaps have been identified an individual must consider outside influences that facilitate participation in continuing education. In the case of a professional, it means harnessing the resources available from professional associations. At the very least, an individual must be aware of the factors that will be conducive and detrimental to the pursuit of continuing education.

(3) Objectives.   An individual, confronted with a long list of identified needs, must set priorities on the basis of desirability and feasibility. The objectives must be formulated in a way so as to spell out desired results that can be evaluated.

(4) Activities. An individual must select and organize learning activities to achieve the objectives. An individual has many options to choose from, including both formal as well as informal activities. They can range from workshops, televised courses and self-instructional modules, to reading and informal discussions. An individual's preference for style of learning counts as much as feasibility in the selection of activities.

(5) Evaluation. At the conclusion of the educational activity, an individual ought to make judgments about its effectiveness in order to improve the educational activity. The judgement is made by comparing expectations and performance based on evidence. Well-formulated objectives can serve as a basis for evidence and making sound judgments.

Almost everyone agrees that education does not define a system that produces individuals who think they know everything, once their formal schooling is completed. One of the greatest achievements of education ought to be a desire to know more. Education should sustain a curiosity that impels the individual to seek out more learning, as one discovers all that there is to know and how little one really knows. Coupled with this kind of hunger for knowledge, education ought to develop in learners an ability to be self-learners; as well as develop a capacity for planning their own programs of learning. Futurologists tell us that our society will not survive without a change in our understanding of education. They insist that we must see education as a lifelong process; a process offering every individual a wide range of options.

REFERENCES

Blaze, Wayne, *et al. Guide to Alternate Colleges and Universities.* Boston: Beacon Press, 1974.

Cross, K. Patricia, Valley, John R., and associates. *Planning Non-Traditional Programs: An Analysis of the Issues for Post-Secondary Education.* San Francisco: Jossey-Bass, 1974.

Diversity By Design. Commission on Non-Traditional Study. San Francisco: Jossey-Bass, 1973.

Drucker, Peter F. *The Age of Discontinuity,* New York: Harper & Row, 1969.

Eis, Jennifer and Ward, Don. *Taking Off.* East Lansing, Michigan: Center for Alternatives In/To Higher Education, 1975.

Gideon, Victor C., *et al. Terminology about Adult/Continuing Education: A Suggested Development Process.* Boston: Systems Management Corporation, November 1971.

Gordon, Edmund W. "Broadening the Concept of Career Education." *IRCD Bulletin,* Vol.9, No. 2, March 1973.

Gould, Samuel B. and Cross, K. Patricia, Editors. *Explorations in Non-Traditional Study.* San Francisco: Jossey-Bass, 1972.

Houle, Cyril O. *The External Degree.* San Francisco: Jossey-Bass, 1973.

Hutchinson, Dorothy J. "The Process of Planning Programs of Continuing Education for Health Managers." *Fostering the Need to Learn.* Monographs and annotated bibliography on continuing education and health manpower. U.S. DHEW, Pub. No. (HRA)74-312, 1974.

Knox, Alan B. "Life-Long Self-Directed Education." *Fostering the Need to Learn.* Monographs and annotated bibliography on continuing education and health manpower. U.S. DHEW, Pub. No. (HRA)74-312, 1974.

Liveright, A.A. *A Study of Adult Education in the United States.* Boston: Center for the Study of Liberal Education for Adults, 1968.

Moses, Stanley. *The Learning Force: An Approach to the Politics of Education.* Syracuse: Educational Policy Research Center, 1970.

Ohliger, John. "Is Lifelong Adult Education a Guarantee of Permanent Inadequacy." Public lecture delivered at Saskatoon, Saskatchewan, March 7 & 8, 1974.

Passett, Barry A. "Motivation and New Careers Training." *New Careers in Action,* Barry A. Passett and Glen M. Parker, Trenton, N.J.: New Jersey Community Action Training Institute, Inc. May 1969.

Tough, Allen. *The Adult's Learning Projects.* Toronto: The Ontario Institute for Studies in Education, 1971.

U.S. Department of Health, Education, and Welfare. *Perspectives of Adult Education in the United States and a Projection for the Future.* Report for the Third International Conference on Adult Education, sponsored by the United Nations Educational, Scientific and Cultural Organization, Tokyo, Japan, July 25-August 7, 1972.

Valley, John R. *Increasing the Options: Recent Development in College and University Degree Programs.* Princeton, N.J.: Educational Testing Service and New York, College Entrance Examination Board, 1972.

Vermilye, D.W., Editor. *Lifelong Learners—A New Clientele for Higher Education.* San Francisco: Jossey-Bass, 1974.

V.

THE EFFECT OF EDUCATIONAL MEDIA AND TECHNOLOGY ON THE CHILD'S LEARNING ENVIRONMENT

By G. F. McVey

The teaching/learning situation has always included some form of instructional media, be it a book, a stick and a smooth area of sand, a chalk board, or projection film. The introduction of these media into the teaching/learning environment inevitably alters the way people function—teachers and students alike. In the past, media use, especially projected media, was infrequent and teachers quite happily relegated its use to the school's "audio-visual room." Today, however, all this has changed. Instructional media has come to play a far more important and significant role at all levels of education. The wave of new or remodeled facilities which emerged in the late 1960s and early 1970s testifies to the growing use of media. Newly designed classrooms with built-in media facilities and environmental controls, exciting learning resource centers, closed-circuit television systems, and local production facilities are all part of the more sophisticated technology of the 1970s.

This growing commitment to media and educational technology is not limited to any specific geographic area or to a particular level of cultural sophistication. For example, media has been grasped by cultures with previously limited awareness of available technology. Major efforts are presently being undertaken by the oil-rich countries of the Middle East and Africa to establish highly technologized educational facilities. In this country, educational media centers are springing up in many farm communities and other rural areas usually thought to be too remote to be influenced by educational trends.

However, we must recognize the fact that constructing new media facilities does not necessarily guarantee the establishment of an active and effective media program. To prove this point, one has only to look at the "skeletons" of sophisticated television and other media facilities which were developed in this country and abroad during the early 1960s. Expensive technology was installed at institutions which were at that time not prepared to provide the support needed to make such facilities functional. During this time, media use in the general classroom fared little better than it did at some new media facilities in colleges and universities. Reports indicate that the early 1960s were not characterized by wide acceptance of media in the classroom. When technology was used, it was primarily as an "add-on" element and not as an integrated component of a curriculum. There were some successful media programs but these understandably were limited to schools where teacher attitude toward media use was high—a feeling obviously not shared by most teachers.

By the middle 1960s the situation began to improve. More teachers were embracing the new educational technologies and the media tools and materials made available principally through government grants to education. During the late 1960s and early 1970s the situation continued to improve. It was during this same period that a number of myths regarding media's potential as a manpower-reducing and cost-savings device were dispelled. First of all, in spite of the dire predictions of media adversaries that the machine would replace the teacher in the classroom, no teacher lost his or her job to the media. Secondly, the claims of technology proponents that educational media would reduce educational costs were also disproved. In their report, Kincaid, *et al.,* reveal:

> Systematic, detailed examinations of overall budgetary costs were undertaken for five representative types of media now available: television (including school-based videocassette libraries), 16mm film, sound filmstrip (individual as well as group modes of presentation), programmed text, and simple forms of computer-based instruction. Results indicated that, at current prices, adding instructional media to the present program of a school can cost anywhere from $0.05 per student-hour for programmed text, through $0.45 per student-hour for individual sound filmstrips, to more than $1.90 per student-hour for computer-based drill and practice. (The latter figure may drop significantly in the next several years.) For comparison, conventional instruction, exclusive of buildings, administration, and custodial functions, costs about $0.55 per student-hour.

The Kincaid report goes on to conclude that given the present organization of school programs where student time in schools is fixed independent of learning, it is likely that the use of media and instructional technology in the classroom will continue to cost more, not less, than traditional teaching programs. Thus, in spite of the fact that present media utilization will not reduce the size of teaching staffs or lower school operating budgets, educational media use continues to grow.

While teacher attitude continues to be the major predictor of the extent of media use, some definite program and organizational trends regarding media utilization have developed. Kincaid, *et al.,* show these trends to include:

(1) Wider use of simpler devices suited for local production and student manipulation, e.g., inexpensive slide and filmstrip production.

(2) Emphasis on technology tailored to the needs of individuals.

(3) More autonomy by the local school in curriculum and budgeting, leading to more decentralized district decisions regarding technology.

As teachers learned to control and develop media for themselves and their students, they began to accept media use more readily. As teachers used media, they became more and more convinced of its effectiveness as a teaching tool. Surprisingly, this commitment to media and technology to improve instruction continues even though we have yet to develop a universally accepted science of instruction. We don't even have a clear understanding of how learning occurs or how fundamental stimuli interact with the learner to produce some desired mental or emotional event. But, just as the operator of a motor vehicle or some other technological tool who has little knowledge of the complex mechanical or electrical operation of his work instrument, the media user can proceed confidently as long as he knows the tool can get the job done. Practical and theoretical questions still remain, however, which must be answered if the media practitioner is to feel confident in using the new media in today's teaching programs as well as in justifying to his or her superiors the budgetary requests to support such programs. These primary questions predominate:

(1) What does the research say which supports the use of media and technology in education?

(2) How can the basic tools of educational media and technology improve learning conditions in the classroom?

(3) What can be done which will promote more effective utilization of educational media in the classroom?

Research and Media Utilization

On the one hand, many studies have concluded that there is "no significant difference" between conventional teaching methods and methods which utilize media. On the other hand, a growing number of studies claim to document the effectiveness of educational media and technology as a teaching tool. Perhaps the divergence in assessment of media effectiveness is due to the multitude of variables that impede research design. For example, program content, conditions under which programs are viewed, and follow-up work in class are just a few of the elements that make measurement of media effectiveness difficult. However, as research techniques improve and familiarity with the subtleties of media grow, more and more reports about the effectiveness of media are coming in. Rather than engage in a prolonged critique of studies which indicate "no significant difference," this chapter will introduce and discuss recent studies that indicate media's effectiveness. Furthermore, it is the author's firm conviction that every teacher should be introduced to the potential of media.

According to John A. Moldstad, director of the Division of Instructional Systems Technology in the Indiana University School of Education, 20 years of research have produced significant evidence to justify the following claims when instructional technology is carefully selected and utilized:

(1) Significantly greater learning often results when media are integrated into the traditional instructional program.

(2) Equal amounts of learning are often accomplished in significantly less time using instructional technology.

(3) Multi-media instructional programs based on a "systems approach" frequently facilitate student learning more effectively than traditional instruction.

(4) Multi-media and audio-tutorial instruction programs are usually preferred by students when compared with traditional instruction.

Moldstad's review encompassed samples of research at all major grade levels. One of the most significant samples included Kelley's (1961) comparative study of the effect of utilizing filmstrips in the teaching of reading to first graders. In this study Kelley found that the youngsters who used filmstrips in their reading program did significantly better in the Gates Primary Reading Tests in word recognition (.01 level of confidence) and sentence reading (.05 level of confidence). He also reported that the teachers participating in the study found that filmstrips improved student interest, stimulated class discussion, helped to fix basic vocabulary, encouraged the timid child, reduced teacher lesson preparation time, and helped in phonetic and structural analysis.

Programmed Instruction

Studies in the area of programmed instruction signal the superiority of this approach over traditional methods even when employed to teach such basic skills as addition and subtraction of fractions. Another study of sixth grade students learning how to spell via programmed instruction and conventional teaching methods revealed gains in learning and/or saved time for the machine-instructed students.

There have been and will probably continue to be arguments as to the efficacy of the programmed instruction format; i.e., linear vs. branching and the use of machines vs. the use of programmed texts. But research results have indicated that any of these formats and approaches will yield greater learning in equal time or equal learning in significantly less time than traditional instructional methods.

Computer-Assisted Instruction

The most recent and sophisticated versions of programmed instruction are the computer-assisted instructional (CAI) programs such as PLATO and TICCIT. Again, as with conventional forms of programmed instruction, time and efficacy gains are in clear evidence.

> One of the most consistent findings with CAI tutorial applications is the marked savings in instructional time along with no loss in post-instructional achievement test performance (Atkinson and Hansen, 1966).

CAI has also shown promise as a diagnostic tool for teachers. A study by Cartwright, Cartwright, and Robine in 1972 demonstrated the relative effectiveness of two forms of a computer-assisted program designed to prepare classroom teachers to engage in the early identification of children with problems expected to adversely affect their school progress. The computer has also been shown to be an excellent tool for diagnosis and mental drill at the elementary school level. Sixth grade arithmetic students using the computer for diagnosis and drill made significantly better progress than their equal counterparts who received traditional classroom drill. Richardson also noted:

> ...it was learned that CAI was most effective when it was integrated into the normal classroom activity. The student's interaction with the terminal must be directly related to and supported by the learning activity in the classroom.

Educational Television

Probably the most researched medium to date has been educational television and the most comprehensive review of the subject is Chu and Schramm's report, *Learning from Television*. Their introductory remarks clearly reflect their positive assessment of television as an educational tool.

> ....The effectiveness of television has now been demonstrated...at every level from pre-school through adult education, and with a great variety of subject matter and method.

Synonymous with the concept of television in education is the Hagerstown, Maryland, television project begun in 1959. Results reported in 1967 after eight years of operation show significant gains for elementary school children. A few examples follow:

(1)   Rural students in grades three through six with Iowa Test of Basic Skills scores a half grade below norm before television, all exceeded the norm after television. Arithmetic scores for fifth graders at the end of one school year showed an average of 1.9 years of growth.

(2)   Sixth grade science students at three different average IQ levels also demonstrated the superiority of television teaching over conventional teaching at all IQ levels. Consistent with other media research, the students with the lowest IQ scores showed the greatest sensitivity to television teaching by evidencing the greatest growth. Television teaching also reduced teacher lesson preparation time and helped in phonetic and structural analyses.

Commercial and educational television broadcast stations have been providing supplementary instructional programs since the mid 1950s. However, the first large-scale experiment in the use of television in teaching reading skills to young children didn't take place until the early 1970s with the Children's Television Workshop production, "The Electric Company." Its evaluation studies included a population of 8363 first through fourth grade children in some 400 classes. They were conducted at the conclusion of its 1971-1972 inaugural broadcast year by the Educational Testing Service and were directed at assessing learning growth on the basis of class performance and not on the performance of individual pupils.

The results of the study indicated that TV viewing classes in the first and second grades made significant gains across nearly the full spectrum of the program's curriculum goals. The program also was shown to have had a significant impact on third and fourth grade viewers although the effect was somewhat less than in the lower grades. The program was shown to have had a similar effect on all groups who viewed TV in school—Spanish speaking, blacks, whites, boys and girls. The program also won favorable reaction from teachers who said they found it useful in teaching and reviewing certain reading skills.

In spite of the success of programs like "The Electric Company," broadcast television has yet to achieve the level of significance in education predicted for it by its proponents. Most of the major problems appear to center on the remoteness of broadcast television's program sources and its fixed scheduling. Ide, in his article "Potentials and Limitations of Television," has noted that while centralized productions are usually high in quality they often lack relevance to the on-going curricula in local schools and that the classroom teacher does not have a real say in their development, presentation and utilization. He noted that:

> ...too often, the teacher has been merely a passive onlooker, a person who directs when the set is to be turned on and off and, if engaged at all, is involved only in conventional pre- and post- telecast activities.

The problem of rigid television broadcast scheduling is no doubt real, but so is the rigidity which characterizes subject and class scheduling in the schools. There is certainly a need for greater flexibility at both ends of the television distribution system. Ide states:

> It has become increasingly clear that if television (broadcast) is to play an important role in education, it will do so either outside existing institutions or within those which have been so altered as to make the best use of it and the other technological media.

To help television reach its potential, Ide calls for greater involvement for the classroom teacher in the development and utilization of broadcast television, greater involvement of the learner in the planning process, and the establishment of television workshops for teachers aimed at developing better utilization skills and a new literacy regarding the media's characteristics.

Multimedia

One of the most exciting and promising forms of educational media, actually an outgrowth of the systems approach toward instruction, has been the experimentation with the ordering and arranging of various single media components into a "combine" known as multimedia. In one of its simplest formats, a multimedia program might include a set of slides, a disc or tape recording, a self-study booklet, a projector and a viewing screen; each component selected on its individual merits, but integrated as a complete package and employed for some desired effective or cognitive learning goal. This media format has usually been associated with higher education programs such as the successful Postlethwait botany series begun in 1961 at Purdue University. However, it has also met with success at the elementary school level and all levels between.

One of the earliest studies to herald the promise of multimedia was that of Louis Romano in 1955 in Whitefish Bay, Wisconsin, where fifth, sixth and seventh grade science students taught via the basic multimedia approach demonstrated statistically significant gains in achievement and improved attitudes over classmates who were taught with conventional classroom materials and techniques. More recently, multimedia kits have been effectively used in gaming and simulation exercises in which the objective is improving a child's problem solving abilities and creative thinking procedures. One such project, "Operation Moon Vigil," sponsored by the Ontario Educational Communications Authority, utilized a series of eight 10-minute videotapes to simulate a crisis on the moon. In their reaction to the crisis, participants were expected to create social institutions in pursuit of a solution to survival.

In one of its more complex forms, multimedia will often include a dozen or more slide projectors, a number of 16mm motion picture projectors, a 360° projection screen, a multichannel audio playback system and a small computer to control the desired ordering and sequencing of the media array. While this latter version is usually found at well funded World's Fairs, more complex multimedia and more sophisticated presentation facilities are becoming more commonplace in today's schools.

The most common multimedia format being used by media specialists today is sometimes referred to by people in the trade as "audible multiple imagery" (AMI). It uses an audio tape for narration and music and sound effects, six slide projectors with three dissolve controls and a programming device to sequence the projectors, and three projection screens for display. The attributes of this multimedia or AMI format include the potential for image comparison, simulation of motion picture effects (at a much lower production cost) and reduced production time using simple and inexpensive conventional production techniques and formats. And since teachers are quite often the producers of such media, its potential as a creative learning activity is high. Trohanis notes:

> To actualize its potential, a wide range of existing and newly produced pictorial and auditory materials can be incorporated for large multiscreen projection. Parts of existing motion picture films, audiotapes, slide sets, and filmstrips can be used. Illustrations from books, magazines or original artwork can be converted easily into 2 x 2 slides by copying the originals.

Interestingly, Trohanis' research indicates that the most effective length of such programs is 10 minutes. This time frame offers the classroom teacher great flexibility in integrating such programs into the regular 50-minute class sessions.

While most of the research studies in the field of educational media and technology deal with the relative effectiveness of the different media, there have been a number of studies which were specifically directed at measuring the effectiveness of the different design and production factors inherent in these media. The pioneering work at the then Pennsylvania State College in the late 1940s and early 1950s by a team of research specialists from various subject disciplines, i.e., psychology, anthropology, etc., headed by Dr. C.R. Carpenter and supported by the resources of the U.S. Naval Special Devices Center, studied most of the conventional media design and production factors from "camera angle," to "optimum viewing distances." A lengthy summary of their findings is contained in the 1000 page 1950 Hoban and Van Ormer report, *Instructional Film Research, 1918-1950.* A succinct review of these and other research findings pertaining to media design effectiveness can be found in Jerrold Kemp's book *Planning and Producing Audiovisual Materials.*

Most similar studies are of the traditional "summative" type; that is, they are concerned with follow-up testing conducted after the product has been produced and utilized in the field. Recently, there has been considerable interest in the promise of "formative" research; research conducted throughout the development and application stages of a media program. Formative research was conducted by the Educational Testing Service for the Children's Television Workshop during the production of "Sesame Street." Here specific learning outcomes and attitudinal changes were found to be directly attributable to specific program design and presentation techniques for gaining attention, encouraging language play, and motivating thinking and learning processes. Continual repetition of short program elements often resulted in learning reinforcement. Readers wishing to know more about this "formative" research and its findings are recommended to Gerald S. Lesser's article, "Learning, Teaching and Television Production for Children: The Experience of Sesame Street," in the May 1972 issue of *Harvard Educational Review*.

The research in the field of educational media and technology reveals its tremendous potential for enriching the learning environment. However, in order to capitalize on this potential the teacher must be made aware of its strengths and weaknesses and must be skilled in the deployment of its tools. Similarly, school administrators should realize that in order to achieve maximum utilization of educational media and technology, they must not only provide the initial media facilities and media resource staff but also establish the means for teachers to sharpen their skills with these new tools. In-house media production and utilization workshops, reward and professional recognition for post-graduate study, adequate media resource budgets and service personnel are recommended. Finally, released time for curriculum development projects and additional flexibility in class structure and scheduling is needed in order to maintain education's continuing drive toward further individualization of curricula.

Educational Media and Improved Learning Conditions

While much has been written concerning the effectiveness of educational media in teaching, little has been written about why it has met with such success. In the section that follows specific instances where audiovisual devices and materials have either proven effective or have shown promise for effectiveness will be cited. A behaviorally oriented rationale for continued and greater use of such media in instructional programs will also be provided.

Educational media in the hands of a competent teacher can promote student interest and enthusiasm for school work by (a) assisting students in their efforts to respond in a learning sequence, (b) reducing the emphasis on verbal communication between teacher and student, (c) providing simulated environmental settings and events, and (d) providing efficient behavioral reinforcers.

Educational media and technology may be employed to perform many functions essential to the teaching-learning process. They may be used as:

(1) Stimulus Intensifiers

(2) Attention Facilitators
(3) Stimulus Generators
(4) Stimulus-Response Recorders
(5) Environmental Simulators

Stimulus Intensifiers

Audiovisual devices intensify stimulus values and improve informa-tion reception. For example, words and numbers displayed by an overhead projector on a white projection screen are projected with greater brightness and contrast than the same symbols printed on a chalkboard and displayed under normal classroom illumination. Research indicates that brightness and contrast are two major factors contributing to symbol and word legibility. Similarly, literature recorded on tape and played back at an increased volume level through a high fidelity sound system is more understandable than literature read at a "normal" voice level by the classroom teacher. It has been shown that word understandability is directly related to signal to background noise ratios. This factor becomes even more important to teachers who con-duct classes in rooms where noise intrusion from external sources, i.e., street traffic, is high or where a particular classroom is too large for good coverage by the teacher's unaided voice.

Attention Facilitators

Children as well as adults tend to orient themselves toward brightly lighted areas. Since projectors brightly illuminate areas for information display, they can help direct the child's attention to it. The same effect has been recently reported where supplementary lighting was used to il-luminate wall-mounted informational displays with the net result being greater attention and achievement by students. Similarly, people tend to orient themselves in the direction of a sound's source. Thus, even when used only as a source of light and sound, audiovisual devices have psycho-physiological value in teaching the child to attend, a major com-ponent of perception and learning.

Attending behavior not only involves the physiological processes of seeing and hearing, but also the psychological processes of looking and listening. And while it is accepted that children generally exhibit similar patterns of attending to auditory and visual events, it has also been established that, for most people, modes of perception and problem solv-ing are individualized. According to Lowenfeld (1959), there are two distinct perceptual types: the "visual" and the "haptic." The visual in-cludes those who instinctively use their eyes to maintain contact with their environment. They tend to transform physical sensation into visual experiences. They react strongly to light stimuli and are visually easily distracted. Good vision is not a prerequisite for this type. In fact, this group generally includes many with the most rudimentary vision. Haptic persons may have excellent vision but instinctively approach everything through the sense of touch, and use their eyes only when compelled by some external force to do so. Educational media, with their multisensory nature, should be of considerable help to the classroom teacher in providing learning experiences which are better matched to a child's modality preference. Audiovisual learning activities, especially those which allow the child to manipulate the equipment and materials, are capable of reaching more children than conventional teaching methods and materials.

Stimulus Generators

Audiovisual equipment and materials give the child practice in coordinating stimulus and response functions. Independent learning devices such as the General Electric Student Response Program Master, combined with a film strip projector, are effective in providing basic experience as well as more advanced language improvement exercises for which they were specifically designed. The overhead projector, used as an "electric chalkboard" with locally produced transparencies, can supply a wide range of opportunities for one-to-one interaction between a responding child and a response-judging and stimulus-reinforcing teacher.

Since skill and discrimination learning is largely non-verbal, visual display equipment is especially valuable to an instructional program. The overhead projector, used in conjunction with "in-house" transparencies, can help the child learn arbitrary visual correspondences such as those which occur between capital and lower case letters or between handwritten and printed letters. Children enjoy manipulating cutouts and tracing or copying figures and symbols on the overhead projector because they can immediately see the effect of their action enlarged on the screen behind them. Such activity also provides a form of reinforcement through immediate display.

The overhead projector is also a very effective tool for developing such complex skills as telling time. This skill involves number recognition, discrimination between lengths of the clock hands, and numeral reading. While such projection transparency kits are available commercially, teachers and students work better with material which they helped design and which resemble the "real" objects found in their everyday environment.

The overhead projector allows the teacher to deviate from the strict textbook approach and adapt instruction to individual needs. It has been shown that the overhead projector can reduce time at the blackboard by 50 percent. The ease of operating an overhead and using transparencies ensures this freedom.

Visual display devices, such as the overhead projector and the slide projector, are also excellent for teaching the child to discriminate between colors, shapes and sizes of objects. Similarly, audio devices, such as tape recorders, record players and commercial or "in-house" produced software can familiarize the student with the important sounds and audio signals characteristic of his environment. Recognition of sounds which connote danger; automobile horns and police sirens, are necessary for the immediate and future safety of all children. A 35mm camera and a portable tape recorder should be particularly useful in this regard, since the sight and sounds of everyday situations can be readily captured by these instruments.

Stimulus-Response Recorders

There are numerous technological devices which may be employed to provide both the stimuli necessary to produce a learning situation for the child and an accurate way for the child and teacher to record and observe responses. When such educational media are used in a student-interactive mode, they are usually called programmed instructional devices. Some of their merits include adaptability to the individual child, immediacy of feedback and reward, and the capability for allowing the student to judge his or her own progress.

These devices range in price and sophistication from $48 for a simple mechanical responder which may be used in conjunction with a conventional AV presentation device, i.e., slide or filmstrip projector; to elaborate computer assisted, Cathode Ray Tube (CRT) display terminals and other electronic programmed instructional devices costing in the thousands of dollars. It is the author's belief, however, that in the hands of a competent and imaginative teacher, conventional "AV Aids" and inexpensive responders may be employed for the above purposes successfully and economically.

Recently, the author observed a teacher using a conventional overhead projector, screen and chalkboard to teach young children the difficult task of handwriting. The only thing new about the approach was a special set of transparencies and an inexpensive (under $40) motion simulator (by Photomotion Corporation) that sat on the overhead projector writing stage. What the child saw, first projected on a matte white screen and then later on white paper taped to the chalkboard, were letters upon which a projected motion pattern was produced. At first, the children followed this moving image at their seats by tracing the animated letters in the air. Then, each took turns tracing the activated letters which were now projected on a sheet of white paper taped to the chalkboard. When this exercise was completed, the children took their finished work back to their desks where they practiced copying the letters now in a conventinal size on another piece of paper. Thus, the children were provided with an excellent learning stimulus, given an opportunity to respond, and were provided with essential practice. At the same time, the teacher had an excellent opportunity to observe and record each child's performance.

The super-8 movie camera is another familiar device which can be used effectively and relatively inexpensively to record learning activities and provide evidence of student's progress to themselves as well as their teachers. The camera can also supply the child with a visual review of first-hand experiences. In the hands of the student, the super 8-camera can record the way he sees things—a valuable record for the teacher's subsequent investigation. This teaching tool is easy to operate, and film processing service (ektachrome film) is quick, inexpensive and readily available. Recent models which also record sound add a further dimension to the potential of this medium.

Another versatile medium which can be used as a stimulus-response recorder is the "video-pak" (video tape recorder and camera). These also range in cost and sophistication. The version which seems to pose the fewest technical and operational restrictions for the classroom teacher is the cassette type. It can be used to observe both child behavior and teacher performance. Videocassettes give the teacher an audiovisual record of the kinds of knowledge and interpretations the child has acquired and the skills he has developed. It also provides the teacher with an insight into the child's thinking, which may underlie his observable behavior. Such a record is important, for the only reliable measure of the relative efficiency and accuracy with which the child has assimilated subject matter is his observable behavior. Thus, video recordings can supply the teacher with a clear assessment of the learning situation. Similarly, a videocassette recording of the teacher's or teacher-aide's performance can give the instructional staff an opportunity to evaluate and improve teaching techniques and procedures.

Being able to match simple tone patterns is critical for the development of vocabulary and articulation skills. Audio programming devices such as the "Audio Card Reader," by Learning Resources Co., can provide such learning experiences via self-instruction. The flash card reader comes equipped with a set of cards on which letters and numbers are boldy printed and the word corresponding to it permanently recorded. After visually recognizing the symbol, the child then identifies the symbol vocally and records his response on the flash card. The child then sends the card through the unit and hears the recorded sound. Thus, visual symbol, recorded vocal equivalent symbol, and the child's own recorded sound—a complete set of correspondences—are readily available for association. Audio active headphones provide a recording capability and keep the playback sound from disturbing other students.

Environmental Simulators

The use of the sound filmstrip and the slide-cassette as self-contained audiovisual instructional units has gained general acceptance in the teaching community. While such automated programs are quite valuable as basic instructional materials, with a small amount of extra photography and audio recording, such equipment can be used to create exciting simulated environmental experiences. A basic simulated environmental display module can be easily constructed by using four slide projectors, a sound sequencing audio recorder, and a wrap-around rear projection screen. The child sits in the center of the box-like screen and witnesses a 360° display of sights and sounds projected by the four projectors and sequenced by the tape recorder. A rear projection screen makes viewing possible even in a moderately lighted room. Earphones keep the audio portion from disturbing students in the classroom who are engaged in other activities.

A 360° projected environmental system has been used with great success at a number of schools across the country. One of the more publicized projects of this type (the environmental simulation theatre at the University of Oregon) is a prototype theatre with five walls (which serve as front projection screens) each measuring 7 feet high by 8 feet wide and connected to create a pentagon shaped enclosure with a diameter of 12 feet. The enclosure is adequate for comfortable viewing by up to 10 students. The presentation system consists of five slide projectors, a tape recorder and a paper tape program synchronizer which is used to automate the program. Commenting on the wide range of experiences this type of facility can provide, Silber and Ewing note:

> In a simulated environment with 360° of sight, sound, smell, touch and taste, children use all their senses and involve themselves in learning as in the real world. Such total environments can maximize learner involvement and outcomes. With the proper ingredients of willingness, ingenuity, adaptability and spirit, environmental simulation could become a teacher's most powerful tool. *All* curriculum areas and interests can use environmental simulation, and students can use *all* their senses and energies in the learning process.

Probably the most sophisticated facility established for this type of learning activity (the "special experiences room," McDonald Elementary School, Warminister, Pa.), is one consisting of a dome-shaped enclosure, a sophisticated panoramic front projection system, and a distributed sound system combined to provide a total environmental surround of projected images, traveling sound, odors and climatic control. While it is used for general instructional enrichment, the room, according to the school's director, Dr. Henry Ray, is especially suited for providing new experiences for perceptually handicapped students—a factor which should be of special interest to today's teachers who are working more frequently with special needs students.

In this section, the author has cited a number of different instances and situations where educational media and technology were used effectively and creatively. He has also identified five major functions or roles which media can assume in the classroom—some conventional and others less conventional. In each case, the overriding assumption has been that teachers would be willing to experiment with new and untried ways of using media to provide their students with distinctive and useful learning experiences.

Improving the Effectiveness of Media Utilization

Thus far we have discussed a number of research findings that support the use of educational media and technology in the classroom. We have also covered some of the important ways that media may be employed as presentation and performance recording devices. In conclusion, some suggestions that should help the teacher use the media in the classroom more effectively will be offered.

Throughout educational media's relatively short history of growth and development, the principal factor which has determined its frequency of use and level of effectiveness has been teacher attitude. There is little question that the teacher candidate who has experienced formal course work and training in educational media selection, production, and utilization is more likely to have a more favorable attitude toward using the new media than his or her counterpart who has not had the benefit of such training. Superintendents of schools are well aware of this and deplore the fact that about 40 percent of today's teachers, nationally, have not taken a course in educational media prior to graduation. They have cited this as one of the major problems in education. Given such critical awareness and concern for this aspect of teacher preparation by the people who occupy key roles in teacher recruitment and placement, it would seem that all prospective teachers would do well to include such course work in their undergraduate programs.

However, teacher attitude toward media is not just something that a newly matriculated undergraduate brings to the school to which he or she has been assigned to teach. It's also something that will develop either positively or negatively, depending upon how easily he or she is able to use the new media. Factors which will affect ease of access and utilization are both human and material. First and foremost, educational materials must be adequate in quantity, good in quality, and accessible with a minimum of "red tape." The reader will find the newly revised ASLA-AECT guidelines, "Media Programs: School and District" (available from the American Librarians Association) a good indicator of what can be expected in the way of media resources in the better schools today. Second, there should be an adequate variety of audiovisual equipment on hand, maintained in good working order. It follows then that there should be on the school staff trained educational media resource people, who in addition to caretaking and maintaining the school's audiovisual materials and equipment, also have enough released time from other school duties to assist teachers and students in the selection, design and production of educational materials.

There must be administrative support both in budget and spirit. The educational climate should be such that teachers are encouraged to use new media in the classroom. The administration should be democratic enough to permit teachers to become involved either individually or in committee in the continuing, systematic selection of educational media for the school's learning resource center. Regularly scheduled professional development in-service workshops should be sponsored and supported by the school administration for its faculty. Such workshops would make teachers more knowledgeable about the new media and provide them with opportunities for sharing with their peers personal accounts of their own media-use success.

The teacher's work schedule should be such that he or she has adequate time to preview and select media for integration into daily teaching programs. Similarly, the student's class schedule should permit time for involvement in creative activities centered around the design and production of instructional materials. Such involvement not only will result in the acquisition of inexpensive, locally produced teaching materials for the classroom, but also in extra-curricular activities which will enrich the student's life. Many of today's highly successful film and television producers and directors are known to have received their first media experiences some 15 or 20 years ago as members of the school's "AV," "TV," or other media "club".

Teachers must be made aware of their power over the commercial producer of educational materials. They should use this power as a lever for effecting positive change. Through their collective efforts they should strive toward making these producers accountable for their products—in quality, substance, and price. They should continually inform these producers of what their media needs are and cite their willingness to assist in the assessment of new products.

Finally, the administration and teaching staff should develop an awareness of what constitutes an environment which supports the effective utilization of educational media and technology. The problem of inadequate or improperly designed educational facilities looms even today in our shiny and colorful new buildings. One recent educational survey noted that about 60 percent of teachers cited poor classroom settings as a major deterrent to their using audiovisual media. It is imperative that teachers develop the ability to recognize and cope with inadequate or poorly designed teaching stations. Unwanted light during film projection, obtrusive noise, inappropriate projector-screen locations and the like are challenges the teacher must meet if they are to, as John Dewey directed over a half century ago, "regulate the environment with reference to its educative effect." A ready and willing resource in this area usually is the school's audiovisual specialist who has had training in educational facilities design and planning. This individual's advice and assistance should be sought out. Quite often the problem can be handled with little money and much ingenuity. Given major facility problems, the teacher and the school media specialist should collectively seek the attention of the school administration, reporting the problem and suggesting measures for its correction.

In this section, the author has offered some suggestions aimed at helping the classroom teacher make more effective use of educational media and technology. It is his hope that the classroom teacher will develop a greater awareness of the interaction between students and the new media, and a greater sensitivity to the interchange between the media, the students and their learning environment.

Educational media and techology offer the teacher limitless potential for broadening his or her participation in the total educational process. Print, television, film, and all other media used in the process of educating students present a vital and continuing challenge for the teacher of today and the teacher of tomorrow.

REFERENCES

Atkinson, R.C. and Hansen, D.N. "Computer-Assisted Instruction in Initial Reading: The Stanford Project." *Reading Research Quarterly,* 1966, 2, pp.5-25.

Ball, S. and Bogatz, G.A. *A Summary of the Major Findings from "Reading with Television: An Evaluation of the Electric Company."* Educational Testing Service, Princeton, New Jersey, March, 1973.

Bugelski, B.R. *The Psychology of Learning Applied to Technology.* Second Edition. Bobbs-Merrill Co., New York, 1971.

Cartwright, C.A., Cartwright, G.P. and Robine, G.G. "CAI Course in Early Identification of Handicapped Children." *Exceptional Children,* 1972, *38,* pp. 453-459.

Chu, G.C. and Schramm, W. *Learning From Television: What the Research Says.* (USOE Contract 2 EFC 70894), Stanford, Cal.: Stanford University, 1967.

Fincher, G.E. and Fillmer, H.T. "Programmed Instruction in Elementary Arithmetic." *Arithmetic Teacher,* 1965, *12,* pp. 19-23.

Godfrey, E.P. *The State of Audio Visual Technology: 1961-1966.* National Education Association, Washington, D.C., 1967.

Ide, T.R. "The Potential and Limitations of Television as an Educational Medium." *Media and Symbols: The Forms of Expression, Communication, and Education,* National Society for the Study of Education, University of Chicago Press, 1974, pp.330-357.

Kelley, T.D. "Utilization of Filmstrips as an Aid in Teaching Beginning Reading." Unpublished doctoral dissertation, Indiana University, 1961.

Kemp, J.E. *Planning and Producing Audiovisual Materials,* Thomas Y. Crowell, N.Y., 1975.

Kincaid, H.V., McEachron, N., and McKinney, D. "Technology in Public Elementary and Secondary Schools: A Policy Analysis." *Educational Media Yearbook, 1974,* Ed. James W. Brown, Bowker Co., New York, 1974, pp. 94-99.

Kryter, K.D. *The Effects of Noise on Man,* Academic Press, New York, 1970

La Guisa, F. and Perney, L. "Brightness Patterns Influence Attention Spans." *Lighting Design and Application,* May, 1973, p.30.

Lowenfeld, V. *The Nature of Creative Activity.* Routledge and Regan Paul, London, 1959.

Lynn, R. Attention. *Arousal and the Orientation Reaction.* Pergamon Press, London, 1966.

Lysaught, J.P. and Williams, C.M. *A Guide to Programmed Instruction.* John Wiley and Sons, New York, 1963.

McVey, G.F. "Legibility and Television Display." *Educational Television,* 1970, pp. 18-23.

____."Learning Experiences via Educational Technology for the EMR." *Mental Retardation,* Dec. 1973, pp.49-53.

Mira, M.P. "Individual Patterns of Looking and Learning Preference among Learning Diabled and Normal Children." *Exceptional Children,* 1968, 34, pp.649-658.

Moldstad, J. "Selective Review of Research Studies Showing Media Effectiveness," *AV Communications Review,* Winter 1974, 22, 4, pp. 387-407.

____. "Some Thoughts on the Past, Present and Future Roles of Instructional Technology." *Viewpoints,* Indiana University, Vol. 51, No. 5, Sept. 1975, pp.1-11.

Porter, D. "Some Effects of Year-Long Teaching Machine Instruction." *The State of the Art: Automatic Teaching,* E. Galanter (Ed.), John Wiley and Sons, New York, 1959, pp. 85-90.

Richardson, W. M. "Research and Implementation of CAI in Elementary and Secondary Schools." *Viewpoints,* Indiana University, 1974, 50, 4, pp. 39-52.

Rocco, J. A. "Developing a Transparency File for Elementary Schools." *Audiovisual Instruction,* 1967, pp. 716-717.

Romano, L. "The Role of Sixteen Millimeter Motion Pictures and Projected Still Pictures in Science Unit Vocabulary Learnings at Grades Five, Six, and Seven." Unpublished doctoral thesis, University of Wisconsin, 1955.

Schramm, W. "The Research on Programmed Instruction: An Annotated Bibliography." U.S. DHEW—O.E., 1964, Contract O.E. 3-16-004.

Silber, K. H. and Ewing, G. W. *Environmental Simulation.* Educational Technology Press, Englewood, New Jersey, 1971.

Silberman, H. F. "Characteristics of Some Recent Studies of Instructional Methods." *Programmed Learning and Computer-Based Instruction,* J.E. Coulson (Ed.), John Wiley and Sons, New York, 1962, pp.13-24.

Trohanis, P. "Classroom Experimentation with Audible Multi-Imagery: Information Learning and Retention Capabilities." Unpublished paper, copyright by author, Chapel Hill, North Carolina, 1972.

Wade, S. Hagerstown, a pioneer in closed-circuit televised instruction. *New Educational Media in Action: Case Studies for Planners—1,* UNESCO, Paris, 1967.

VI.

CAREER EDUCATION
By David C. Gardner

Several weeks ago my wife and I spent an evening with some new friends. We learned that their eldest son, Benjamin, had refused to enroll in college as planned. Ben had just graduated, with honors, from a college-preparatory program in a public high school. Not only that, he had refused to even consider looking for employment and the summer was nearly over. From our discussion with his parents, it soon became obvious that their son had a limited knowledge of the many career possibilities open to him. Also, Ben had failed to acquire appropriate attitudes toward work and was "turned off by the whole job scene." As far as Ben was concerned, school and work were both "irrelevant."

Ben is typical of Americans attempting to deal with rapidly changing technology, shifting labor markets, and conflicting values about work and society.

Take the case of Mary, for instance. Not too long ago, I spent several hours with her in my office. Mary was a very unhappy college senior who explained to me that no one wanted her as an employee. Mary could not understand why no one would hire her when she would very shortly be receiving a college degree in foreign languages. When I explained to her that the job market for foreign language graduates was limited and, at the minimum, required that she be fluent in several languages, she began to complain that no one had told her all this earlier. Mary said that she had always believed that a college degree would guarantee her a good job. Mary learned very quickly that a college degree is no longer a ticket to a good job. She also learned that her college program had failed to provide her with the necessary skills (e.g., fluency in several foreign languages) for employment in her chosen field.

A similar difficulty faced Janice, who had recently earned a doctorate in medieval history from a midwestern university. Janice dropped into my office seeking help in finding a job. She had no idea of how to go about looking for employment and had never written a resume. But she was sure that she didn't want to work in her field. "Anyway," she said, "there are no jobs." Further, she felt the only salvation for her was to get a practical degree like a Master of Business Administration or "something similar." Janice thought she might like to be an office manager but was afraid to acquire the basic skills. Janice believed that a woman who could type and file was destined never to be more than a secretary.

These cases illustrate the many real life crises facing thousands of Americans, young and old, across the country today. These examples are also representative symptoms of an educational process which has failed to provide for the work dimensions of our culture. One comprehensive response to this failure is "career education."

A Reform Movement

Career education is a reform movement in American education, a proposal for reform which offers "...a comprehensive and long-range solution to many of America's social problems" (Gardner, 1973). It is a reform movement which, according to Kenneth Hoyt, associate commissioner of Career Education, United States Office of Education (USOE), seeks to correct some of the prime criticisms (failures) of American education. As you read the USOE list of prime criticisms, study them carefully. You no doubt will discover that the problems of Janice, Mary, and Ben are represented. Many of you will also recognize problems facing people you know: friends, relatives, and acquaintances.

USOE List of Prime Criticisms:

(1)   Too many persons leaving our educational system are deficient in the basic academic skills required for adaptability in today's rapidly changing society.

(2)   Too many students fail to see meaningful relationships between what they are being asked to learn in school and what they will do when they leave the educational system. This is true of both those who remain to graduate and those who drop out of the educational system.

(3)   American education, as currently structured, best meets the educational needs of that minority of persons who will some day become college graduates. It fails to place equal emphasis on meeting the educational needs of that vast majority of

students who will never be college graduates.

(4) American education has not kept pace with the rapidity of change in the post-industrial occupational society. As a result, when worker qualifications are compared with job requirements, we find over-educated and under-educated workers are present in large numbers. Both the boredom of the over-educated worker and the frustration of the under-educated worker have contributed to growing worker alienation in the total occupational society.

(5) Too many persons leave our educational system at both the secondary and collegiate levels unequipped with the vocational skills, the self-understanding and career decision-making skills, or the work attitudes that are essential for making a successful transition from school to work.

(6) The growing need for and presence of women in the work force has not been reflected adequately in either the educational or the career options typically pictured for girls enrolled in our educational system.

(7) The growing needs for continuing and recurrent education of adults are not being met adequately by our current systems of public education.

(8) Insufficient attention has been given to learning opportunities which exist outside the structure of formal education and are increasingly needed by both youth and adults in our society.

(9) The general public, including parents and the business-industry-labor community, has not been given an adequate role in the formulation of education policy.

(10) American education, as currently structured, does not adequately meet the needs of minority or economically disadvantaged persons in our society.

(11) Post high school education has given insufficient emphasis to educational programs at the sub-baccalaureate degree level (Hoyt, 1975, pp. 1-2).

Career education can be viewed as a response to these criticisms of American education. While not the only possible response, career education is a unique and comprehensive response.

Career education is a reform movement which is on the minds of many educators, students, and parents. It is also a major concern of many community, business, industrial, and labor leaders. Career education is a reform movement unlike any reform movement in our country's educational history. In just the short period since Sidney Marland, Jr., (then U.S. commissioner of education) announced career education as a priority area of the USOE in early 1971, the efforts of the many supporters of the movement culminated in the establishment of an Office of Career Education in Washington, congressional legislation on career education, the publication of a policy paper on career education by the USOE (Hoyt, 1975), and the founding of the National Association of Career Education by a group of career education practitioners in 1974 (Gardner and Smith, 1975). In the context of our work-oriented culture, the basic appeal of career education's philosophy, conceptual framework, and its promise, may at least partially explain its remarkable acceptance by laymen and professionals alike.

Definition of Career Education

Career education has probably had nearly as many definitions as practitioners. Marland (1974) devotes an entire chapter in his new book to defining career education. The following definition, which appears in both the first and second editions of a best selling career education book by Kenneth Hoyt and others, is probably the most quoted definition:

> Career education is the total effort of public education and the community to help all individuals become familiar with the values of a work-oriented society, to integrate these values into their personal value systems, and to implement these values in their lives in such a way that work becomes possible, meaningful, and satisfying to each individual (Hoyt, *et al.,* 1974, p. 15).

In the recently published U.S. Office of Education (USOE) policy paper on career education Hoyt (1975) further defines career education as:

> ...the totality of experiences through which one learns about and prepares to engage in work as part of her or his way of living (p. 4).

The USOE definition is further clarified by defining such key words as *career, education,* and *work.*

Work is defined as:

> ...conscious effort, other than that involved in activities whose primary purpose is either coping or relaxation, aimed at producing benefits for oneself and/or oneself and others (p. 3).

A *career* is seen as the "...totality of work one does in his or her lifetime", and *education* as the "...totality of experiences through which one learns" (p. 3).

In interpreting these and other definitions related to career education, there are certain concepts most definers agree on. The first is that career education should be viewed as a developmental approach in its process and practice and that it is applicable to all persons of all ages, from early childhood through adult years. Another is that career education should be multi-institutional. The responsibility for career education implementation must be shared by the family, school, community, business, labor, and industry.

Career education is viewed by most definers as an integrating or "fusion" medium and not as an add-on item in the curriculum. Many definers go to great lengths explaining that career education is not synonomous with vocational education or with counselling. Yet both vocational guidance and vocational education are considered by all career educators as important components in any career education model.

Most career educators would support the notion that a fundamental principle in career education is that:

> ...all educational experiences, curriculum, instruction, and counselling should be geared to preparing each individual for a life of economic independence, personal fulfillment, and an appreciation for the dignity of work (Worthington, 1972, p. 213).

Marland (1974) points out that in the final analysis, it is the individual, the teacher, the school administrator, the school system, the community, *those practicing career education,* who will do the defining.

Basic Principles of Career Education

The following principles underlie the basic approaches and objectives of career education. These are paraphrased from a 1972 USOE publication entitled *Career Education: Handbook for Implementation* (pp. 7-8).

(1) Since a key objective of all education should be preparation for successful working careers, then:

(a) Every teacher in every course will emphasize, where appropriate, the relationship between subject matter and its possible contribution to a successful working career.

(b) Teachers and the school system will adopt hands-on, occupationally-oriented experiences as methods for teaching academic subjects, as well as for motivating students to learn abstract content.

(2) Since career preparation involves the acquisition of appropriate work attitudes and human relations skills, familiarity with the world of work and alternate career choices, and the mastery of actual job skills, the classroom is viewed as only one of many learning environments in career education. Learning should also take place in the community, the home, and on the job.

(3) Since career education is seen as developmental in nature, a "cradle to the grave approach", it must provide for (a) early childhood career education, (b) career education during the regular school years, and (c) open entry/exit programming for youth and adults who wish to acquire experience and then re-enter the system at any time for further education and job skill upgrading. The open entry/exit principle includes revitalizing adult workers for productive use of leisure time and retirement years.

(4)   Another important principle places the responsibility on the schools to:

> ...stick with the youth until he has feet on the career ladder, help him get back on the ladder if his foot slips, and be available to help him onto a new ladder at any point in the future when the old one proves to be too short or unsteady (Evans, *et al.,* 1973, p. 13).

These and other principles and practices of career education are based in part on research findings, and in part on professional judgements (clinical hunches) and observations. They have been restated as 25 testable hypotheses under the heading "Programmatic Assumptions of Career Education" in the USOE policy paper on career education (Hoyt, 1975, p. 5).

Some examples:

> (1)   If students can see relationships between what they are being asked to learn in school and the world of work, they will be motivated to learn more in school.

> (6)   Work values, a part of one's personal value system, are developed to a significant degree during the elementary school years and are modifiable during those years.

> (12)   The same general strategies utilized in reducing worker alienation in industry can be used to reduce worker alienation among pupils and teachers in the classroom.

> (20)   Relationships between education and work can be made more meaningful through infusion into subject matter than if taught as a separate body of knowledge (Hoyt, 1975, pp. 5-7).

The testing of the USOE's 25 programmatic assumptions of career education through the implementation and evaluation of career education programs is to some extent underway in a growing number of communities across the country. For the programmatic assumptions of career education to be fully tested some basic changes in our educational system must occur. Dr. Hoyt has outlined some of the major changes called for in an essay entitled "Career Education: Myth or Magic". Some examples:

> (1)   The elimination of the concept "school dropout" by establishing an open-entry/exit system of education in the U.S.A.

> (2)   The increased use of the project approach to instruction. This approach emphasizes individualization of instruction and small class size.

> (3)   The development of a new system for granting educational credit to students for tasks performed outside schools under the supervision of non-certified teachers.

> (4)   The establishment of comprehensive counselling, placement, career guidance, and follow-up services for all youth and adults whether enrolled in school or not.

(5) The adoption of performance evaluation as the primary method for measuring educational outcomes.

(6) The use of educational facilities on a 12-month basis for increased efficiency in training youth and adults. Such an approach would allow for flexible scheduling of programs and permit teachers to acquire experience outside the field of education (Hoyt, 1973, pp. 29-30).

Career Education in Practice

Career education "models" are being developed at both state and local levels with varying degrees of definition (and funding) across the country. The federal government has established four models and, according to D. Smoker "...has allocated millions of dollars to research and development efforts..." in career education.

By far the most widely discussed model funded by the USOE is the School-Based Comprehensive Career Education Model. The school-based model provides career education for students in a K-Life educational system. This model will be described in more detail in the section below.

Other models funded by USOE are (1) the Experience-Based Model, (2) the Home/Community-Based Model, (3) the Rural-Residential Model.

The Experience-Based Model (EBCE)

At first labeled the Employer-Based Model, EBCE offers an alternative sytem of secondary education to youth from 13 to 18 years old. According to an undated brochure entitled "The Community is the Teacher" published by the National Institute of Education (NIE), students in Philadelphia, Pennsylvania; Charlestown, West Virginia; Oakland, California; and Tigard, Oregon; have been "exchanging ideas with and learning from adults in the everyday world" (p. 2). On page 4 of the NIE brochure, the EBCE model is further described as pulling together the:

...many innovations transforming American education today under various names— schools without walls, action learning, individually prescribed instruction, competency-based certification, survival education.

In the 1975 NIE booklet the EBCE model is distinguished from traditional work/study programs on the basis that the program does not emphasize vocational skills per se, that EBCE is unpaid experience, that EBCE includes career exploration and employer-site rotation procedures, that EBCE uses experiential education for conveying learning in academic areas, that EBCE allows a greater student role in shaping a personalized educational plan and, lastly, the EBCE is not targeted to dropouts, disadvantaged, or other specific populations (p. 3).

The Home/Community-Based Model

The Home/Community-Based Model was originally "conceived as a system for delivering educational services to the home" (Smoker, 1974). In operation in Providence, Rhode Island, since October, 1972, under the auspices of the Educational Development Corporation in Newton, Massachusetts, this NIE sponsored project has focused on providing career counselling services by telephone for adults on a paraprofessional basis. The project has also operated a Resource Center that provides career-related materials for and about adults. The project has also published five manuals, annotated bibliographies, and a film. The Home/Community-Based Model:

> ...has served over 5000 men and women, aged 16 to 70, with different employment histories, education, economic levels, and career aspirations. Because the target group has been defined as home-based...most of the project's clients have been women (EDC, 1975, p. 3).

Rural-Residential Model

According to Marland (1974) the Rural-Residential Model, being developed by the Mountain-Plains Education and Economic Development Program, Inc., focuses on:

> ...chronically underemployed multi-problem rural families. It represents a "total" intervention in that it attempts to influence all significant activities of the family, not only the education-related activities. The major goal is to make the family unit economically viable through career counselling, training, remedial education and guidance for children; homemaking and family development skills for the parents and job placement (p. 284).

Heads of households are expected to participate a minimum of 40 hours per week in the program; spouses may participate 20-40 hours per week. Program areas include home management, health education, counselling, career guidance, foundation education, and occupational preparation in carpentry, plumbing, electrical, air conditioning, lodging and food services, transportation, office education, marketing and distribution.

The School-Based Comprehensive Career Education Model(CCEM)

The objective of this USOE model can best be described as an attempt to reform the curriculum of the established public school system. The prime contractor for the CCEM is the Center for Vocational and Technical Education at Ohio State University. The center has selected six local school districts as sites for field testing and development of career education materials: Mesa, Arizona; Pontiac, Michigan; Hackensack, New Jersey; Jefferson County, Colorado; Los Angeles, California; and Atlanta, Georgia.

In addition to these federally-funded models, a number of states and many local school systems have developed (or are developing) their own models of career education. The USOE has maintained that the basic form of career education will have to be developed at the local and state levels. There is little doubt, however:

> ...that the activities and findings of these multimillion dollar projects...will provide significant inputs to the process of defining and implementing career education....Certainly, for anyone interested in career education, the models merit serious attention (Smoker, 1974, p. 28).

Practitioners have generally utilized a four or five stage model with some stages overlapping one another. Even a cursory review of texts in the field of career education would indicate that a very popular mode is the pyramid-like model (inverted or upright). Frequently illustrated models appear to be the "USOE Inverted Pyramid" and "The Oregon Way." Figure 1 is illustrative of most models.

The Cluster Concept

One important challenge in implementing curriculum reform in the career education school-based model is the basic problem of how to deal with the more than 45,000 jobs listed in the *Dictionary of Occupational Titles* and the Department of Labor catalog (Weagraff, 1975). The most reasonable approach is to group jobs into related, broad clusters which can form the framework around which curriculum and instructional activities can function.

While there are a number of cluster schemes, the most widely accepted system among career educators is the 15-cluster system developed

FIGURE 1. ILLUSTRATIVE STAGES OF
SCHOOL-BASED MODELS

STAGE I

Usually referred to as the Career Awareness Stage. Some models grade K-4, K-5, or K-6. Concerned with self-awareness of students. No attempt to "train." The Oregon Model is K-6. In this model, students are expected to develop awareness of many careers available, awareness of self in relation to careers, respect and appreciation for all workers in all fields, and to make tentative choices of career clusters to explore in mid-school years. General approach has been to integrate career awareness into the existing curriculum, (e.g. reading, science, math, and social studies). Other strategies include examining the community's world of work through guest speakers and field trips.

STAGE II

Commonly referred to as the Career Exploration Stage. Begins around grades 5 or 6 and extends into the middle school or junior high school. Students begin to explore several of the 15 USOE occupational clusters. Oregon model extends from grades 7-10. Students' objectives include exploration of key occupational areas, assessment of career interests and abilities, development of awareness of relevant decision-making factors, gaining experience in meaningful decision making, development of tentative occupational plans; students arrive at tentative career choice. Students explore the world of work and receive "hands-on" experiences. Also can involve field trips, career resource centers, career laboratories (simulations), paid and unpaid work experience, etc.

STAGE III

Generally called the Career Preparation Stage. Approximately grades 9-12. Major goal is for students to develop either entry-level job skills or be prepared for advanced occupational training. Ideal model eliminates college preparatory, vocational, and general tracks. The Oregon Model encompasses grades 11-12. Oregon students are expected to acquire entry-level skills or be prepared for advanced vocational training, develop appropriate job attitudes, and obtain work experience. An often cited example of an outstanding secondary program at this stage is the Skyline Development Center in Dallas, Texas.

STAGE IV

Sometimes called the Career Specialization Stage. Portions of this stage are sometimes combined with portions of Stage III. Many models also include adult and continuing education education (a possible Stage V) in this stage. The concentration here is on advanced career preparation above the high school level. Includes apprenticeships, associate degree programs, vocational certificate programs, university bachelors and advanced degree programs, etc. One concept is that this stage can take place at any age and may involve alternate periods of work and study. In the Oregon Model the emphasis is on developing specific occupational preparation and knowledge in a special job area; provisions for forming meaningful employer-employee relationships and learning skills for retraining and upgrading.

by the USOE. Under each cluster all types of jobs are included from entry level through technical, skilled and professional level positions. The USOE clusters are:

Agri-Business and Natural Resource Occupations

Business and Office Occupations

Communication and Media Occupations

Construction Occupations

Consumer and Homemaking Occupations

Environmental Control Occupations

Fine Arts and Humanities Occupations

Health Occupations

Hospitality and Recreation Occupations

Manufacturing Occupations

Marine Science Occupations

Marketing and Distribution Occupations

Personal Service Occupations

Public Service Occupations

Transportation Occupations

Following the multi-stage school based model, the school system can use the cluster approach as a framework for orienting students to careers and as a focal point for instructional and curriculum development activities. In the elementary grades, students study all clusters. In middle or junior high school, students usually choose five or six clusters to explore. Early in high school, a student may deal with one or two areas, and by the last two years in high school concentrate on career preparation in one cluster.

By 1976, according to Dr. Marland (1974),

...major curricular development will have been completed for all fifteen clusters. These curricula are designed, consistent with the career education theory, to interface with the corresponding academic programs. They will cover the span of related academic content from kindergarten through grade twelve (p. 306).

Making it Work: Examples

Ben's sister, Louise, is in a second grade classroom where the teacher tries to make all appropriate activities relate to the world of work. Louise's teacher has attended several workshops on career education and receives consultation from the elementary career education coordinator. Nearly half of the parents in Louise's class have participated in various career education activities.

Presently, the class is completing a unit on the Postal Service. Among the activities completed and/or planned are field trips to small post office branches in preparation for a trip to the main post office, a lesson on the history of the postal service, interviews with their own mailmen, viewing films and filmstrips on various postal service occupations, role playing different postal service occupations, and so forth.

Louise and her classmates follow the same content curriculum as previous elementary classes: language arts, social studies, science, arithmetic, art, and music. However, correlating activities in each content area are integrated with the unit. For instance, students read stories related to post office workers and are making a picture dictionary of new words introduced in the unit (language arts). They also have used a scale to practice weighing packages of different weights and have computed the costs for mailing each package (arithmetic).

Mary's brother, Bill, is a senior in a regional comprehensive high school. Bill has worked two summers in a service station and continues to work several evenings and Saturdays. He receives academic credit for this experience and is supervised by a placement coordinator. During the school year he spends alternate weeks in an automotive technology shop and in academic classrooms under the supervision of an interdisciplinary team of teachers. Each teacher attempts to individualize classroom activities and assignments to relate to Bill's interest in the automotive field. Bill's boss has already promised him a full-time job upon graduation. Bill plans to take management courses at a community college at night while he works full-time. His long-range goal is to own his own service station.

Career Education and You

How total implementation of the USOE career education models across the United States may affect your life largely depends upon the timing, sequencing, and models adopted in your state. In a much broader sense, however, the implications of career education for you are tied to the many roles you will play (and are playing) in our society in the years to come. Below are some examples of what the career education movement may mean to you, now and in the future.

As a College Student

One of the more obvious effects of career education infusion into the college curriculum (or any curriculum) will be the elimination of many of the assignments commonly labeled "irrelevant" by students. (e.g. the other day I ran into a friend of mine who had recently begun doctoral studies at a nearby university. I asked him how it felt to be in school after ten years of working as a professional in the field. He said he liked the idea of updating his skills but still couldn't get used to doing school assignments that had no meaning to him as a professional. I explained that if his course instructor had used a career education approach in making that same assignment, the same content would have been covered in a more meaningful way for each individual student, including my friend.)

Other changes in the college curriculum may include (1) lectures on the career implications of each course's content; (2) increased career placement and career counselling services provided by the college and (3) increased multi-dimensional career training programs and options. These changes should not only bring "relevance" to the college classroom for you but would also increase your chances for (1) making appropriate career choices and (2) for obtaining a job upon graduation in the field in which you have been trained.

As an Adult Worker

You live in a rapidly changing world, a world in which each technological breakthrough carries the potential of making thousands of trained workers obsolete almost overnight. When coupled with such factors as rising inflation, high professional unemployment and recessionary cycles, individual career choice and job selection problems are indeed complex.

As an adult worker you may be called upon to change the way in which you earn your living several times during your lifetime. Under the career education system, you will be able to return to school or enter a training program for job retraining through an easy-entry/exit system. At the end of your training period, you will be provided with efficient career counselling and placement services which will expedite your re-entry into the professional labor force.

As an adult worker you may also be called upon to assist in training youth and adults to work in your chosen field. Your participation in the educational process may include (1) supervising a student-worker, (2) guest speaking or teaching at a school or college or, (3) perhaps serving as a technical consultant to schools for curriculum development and updating.

As a Parent

The opportunities for parents to participate in career education are many. Among the tasks you may be called upon to perform are (1) assisting your child's teacher in supervising children on field trips to business and industry (2) serving on an advisory board for curriculum development and updating (3) providing opportunities for your own children to participate in exploratory activities in the world of work beyond those provided by the school (4) participating as a volunteer during "career days" held by your child's school, and (5) serving as a guest speaker in classrooms several times each year.

Regardless of how you participate in the career education movement, whether as a student, worker, or parent, you may begin to understand what John Dewey said a long time ago (1889), that "It is through what we do in and with the world that we read its meaning and measure its value" (p.42). When you volunteer in that classroom or help train a young person on-the-job, you may feel as John Dewey felt about those who objected to bringing the world of work and academics together:

> When occupations in the school are conceived in this broad and generous way, I can only stand lost in wonder at the objections so often heard, that such occupations are out of place in the school...It sometimes seems to me that those who make these objections must live in quite another world. The world in which most of us live is a world in which everyone has a calling and occupation, something to do. Some are managers and others are subordinates. But the great thing for one as for the other is that each shall have had the education which enables him to see within his daily work all there is in it of large and human significance (Dewey, 1899, p.45).

REFERENCES

Career Counselling for Adults: An Overview of the Home- and Community- Based Career Education Project. Newton, Massachusetts: Educational Development Center, Inc., U.S. Government Printing Office, 1975.

Career Education: A Handbook for Implementation. Maryland State Board of Education, Washington, D.C.: U.S. Government Printing Office, 1972.

The Community Is the Teacher. Washington, D.C.: National Institute of Education, U.S. DHEW, 1975.

Dewey John. "The School and Society" (1899). Dworkin, M.S. *Dewey on Education.* New York: Teachers College Press, Columbia University, 1959, pp.33-49.

Evans, R., Hoyt, K., and Mangum, G. *Career Education in the Middle/Junior High School.* Salt Lake City: Olympus Publishing Company, 1973

Gardner, D.C. "Career Education in Our Town?" *College Student Journal,* 1973, 7 (3), pp.73-77.

Gardner D.C., and Smith, K.E. The National Association of Career Education. *Illinois Career Education Journal,* July, 1975.

Hoyt, K. B. "Career Education: Myth or Magic?" *NASSP Bulletin, 57,* March, 1973, (371), pp. 22-30.

_____. *An Introduction to Career Education: A Policy Paper of the U.S. Office of Education.* (DHEW Publication No. OE75-00504). Washington, D.C.: U.S. Government Printing Office, 1975.

Hoyt, K.B., Evans, R.N., Mackin, E.F., and Magnum, G.L. *Career Education: What It Is and How to Do It.* Salt Lake City: Olympus Publishing Company, 1972, 2nd Edition, 1974.

Marland, S.P. *Career Education: A Proposal for Reform.* New York: McGraw Hill Book Company, 1974.

Smoker, D. *Career Education: Current Trends in School Policies and Programs.* Arlington, Virginia: National School Public Relations Association, 1974.

Weagraff, P.A. "Career Education Curriculum Development Using the Cluster Concept." Wigglesworth, D.C. (Ed.). *Career Education.* San Francisco: Canfield Press, 1975, pp.109-114.

Worthington, R.M. "Home-Community Based Career Education Model." *Educational Leadership,* December, 1972, *30,* (3), p.213.

VII.

SPECIAL EDUCATION ISSUES IN THE SEVENTIES

By Sue Allen Warren

Decisions about topics to be included in any discussion of current issues in special education will depend, in part, on one's definition of special education, on whether only controversial issues are included, and on one's view of the current scene. For example, one issue at this time concerns the selection of those persons who might be legitimately served in special education programs: Adults? Infants? Poor children? Those with reading problems only? Different professionals have different answers.

Consideration of what special education is (or is not) seems to be the first questions. Although there may be some disagreement by others in the field, I will use the term as it is most commonly used by special educators. Special education will be used to describe educational services provided to school age children who require some kind of "extra" educational provisions because of marked difference from other children in sensory, intellectual, communication, motor, or interpersonal skills. Such "different" children are defined and so classified because they are not able to function adequately and profit sufficiently from the regular education programs available to other children. With this definition, one would include for special education services those students who are sometimes referred to as mentally retarded, learning disabled, visually handicapped, hearing handicapped, speech disordered, emotionally disturbed (behaviorally disordered) or suffering from a chronic illness which interferes with their potential for adequate functioning in regular classrooms under ordinary circumstances.

Not all of the current important issues in special education are controversial. However, there are enough controversial ones to warrant limiting this discussion to them. In order to decide which were the most urgent of the controversial ones, a number of areas were surveyed. An accounting of recent books and journal articles on various topics was made. Themes of national conventions and regional meetings of major organizations in the field were recorded. Recent legislative and adversary proceedings were reviewed. And major concerns of national organizations of professions as indicated by position papers and other publications were studied.

After the survey, it appeared that the major controversial issues today include:

How Special is Special Education?
Right to Education
Mainstreaming and Normalization
Labels and Classification
Early Identification
Techniques of Instruction
Assessments and Uses of Tests

These are the issues which are debated in such journals as *Exceptional Children* and *Mental Retardation*. These are the topics of papers presented at annual meetings of the Council for Exceptional Children, the Association for Children with Learning Disabilities, the American Association on Mental Deficiency, and the relevant divisions of the American Psychological Association.

These are not necessarily new. Some have been debated for years and the pendulum swings from side to side. Some seem to temporarily die down, only to rise again a few years later. Perhaps this happens because many of these issues are related to values rather than to research findings only. Perhaps the special education issues reflect our current outlook, with national problems or issues reflecting themselves in this focus. Whatever the origins, these are the topics.

How Special Is Special Education?

In the decade of the sixties, some of the national leaders in special education began to question the degree to which special education is "really" special. One even made the remark in a major presentation at a national convention that special education is neither "special" nor "education." There were tirades about the "watered-down" regular curricula and complaints that there is really nothing at all unusual or special about such offerings. Most of the debate included a large measure of talk about the so-called "efficacy" studies on special classes. Since retarded children make up a great proportion of special class placements and since they are particularly vulnerable in regular classes, the various studies of the effectiveness of their special classes became a focal point of arguments. Although special classes had begun in the United States as early as 1896 (Providence, R.I.), they did not become widespread until the second and third quarters of this century. The very rapid spread of special classes in America has been linked to the development of intelligence tests, to compulsory education which kept in schools many "poor" students who would have otherwise dropped out, and to an increased concern for handicapped individuals following our first maiming war, World War II. The spread was, for whatever reasons, very rapid.

Even with the marked increase in programs for disabled children, the national figures indicate that never more than half the children in need of special education (as projected from estimated numbers based on regional surveys) were ever in special programs of any type prior to 1970. Since projections of numbers in need of service were based on "guesstimates" from small surveys of populations which may not have been typical, they were subject to question. For example, the prevalence of emotionally disturbed children has been estimated from about 2 percent to over 15 percent of the school population; such an estimate probably tells more about the quality of definitions of emotional disturbance than it tells about numbers of distressed children in the country. It tells nothing at all about the quality of programs for those children who were receiving service.

In the early thirties, efforts were made to determine the value of public school special programs for the handicapped, at that time almost exclusively carried on in special (segregated) classes. Those and later studies were criticized for poor research design, and failure to control for selection factors. Studies in the fifties and later attempted to attend to research design problems. Thurstone used large numbers and measured progress across time; Johnson and Capabianco, studying programs for trainable retarded children, used differing settings and amounts of time in class; and Hottel and Dunn used children at home and in classes in Tennessee as subjects. A California study investigated the results of special training of children in programs and not in programs in institutions and in the community. Adding together the results of different studies which controlled for different factors, the detractors of special education came to the conclusion that special education had not been demonstrated to be effective. (They did not, however, add in those early studies which had shown quite clearly that retarded and disturbed children tend to be rejected by their age peers who are not handicapped. Neither did they use studies showing that occupational success was greater for those educated in special programs than for similar students in regular classes without special provisions.)

Is special education special? I think so. It is special if one views it as special provisions for school children rather than as "something special and unusual." In fact, any child on crutches must have special provisions made for him if he is to function in a public school building. Any child whose vision is no better than 20/70 corrected must have special equipment and materials if he is to reach maximal potential. A retarded child who must make many attempts to consistently recognize the combination of *w-a-s* as *was* and not *saw,* needs special treatment.

Special education is also education. A great debate raged over whether teaching a child was education or training if a child was merely being taught self-help skills or given aid in learning to hold his spoon. Although professions develop esoteric meanings for ordinary words, the debates over whether the "training" of handicapped children is "education" were pointless. A few minutes with Webster could have eliminated hours of discussion. The definition of education is given as "to provide schooling for, to develop mentally or morally especially by instruction." Training is defined as "to teach so as to make fit, qualified, or proficient." Neither definition requires, as some critics of school programs for the handicapped seemed to insist, that the training or education must result in self-sufficiency and productiveness as an adult.

Others may not agree, but I think that special education is both special and education.

Right to Education

The right to education is a term now in use to refer to the numerous class action suits in which parents of handicapped children have demanded educational provisions for their children. This topic is closely allied to the discussion of what education really is. The first and most famous of the suits is known as PARC (Pennsylvania Association for Retarded Children) vs. Pennsylvania. This suit was entered in 1971 on behalf of a child who had been denied schooling on the grounds that she was too retarded to profit from education. Many state laws and regulations specifically included the words "able to profit" to determine which children should be admitted to free public education systems. Although many states passed legislation that provided school programs for trainable retarded children during the fifties and sixties, those laws were almost always permissive and not mandatory; thus, most schools did not offer such classes. Finally, PARC filed suit in a Pennsylvania federal court. That suit was "won" in the sense that the state of Pennsylvania consented to provide education, but the fact that it was a consent decree prevented the case from going to the U.S. Supreme Court.

Nevertheless, other states and their administrators, some with suits entered against them, recognized the handwriting on the wall. Across the nation agreements were made that educational opportunities for all types of children, handicapped or not, must be provided. Just how many children are still without appreciable service these few years later is unknown, but they are probably very numerous. Public schools and their personnel are not (or do not feel) equipped to help such severely handicapped children. Many professionals active in the field for years still think that special education is not an appropriate answer. Court suits have been won and orders have been given. Resistance, confusion, and debate remain.

There are those who feel that court action is not necessarily the best or most effective means of gaining public education services for handicapped children. Their argument is that better programs are likely to be provided in greater numbers and with greater willingness if school personnel (especially administrators and school boards) are convinced that it is their responsibility and that they can do it well. The position is that one first seeks to convince those in responsible positions that they should help provide for all children in need of services. When an approach to administratively responsible persons does not work because of inadequate legislative enabling acts, the second approach is to those who make laws. The new Massachusetts Chapter 766 legislation is an illustration of this approach. That law makes broad provisions for children "with special needs" because of sensory, intellectual, motor, or other disabilities. More important, it encourages a wide variety of services and recommends that the children be educated in an environment as nearly "normal" as practical. This Massachusetts special education law is a prototype and a landmark.

It is also controversial. Taxpayers have criticized it because it is expensive at a time when taxes are rising in the state and the new special education law provides a ready "whipping boy" on which to place blame. Some special educators have criticized it because they believe that it does not have a sound experimental basis. For example, little is known about the overall advantages and disadvantages of integration of handicapped children. This criticism has some merit because the studies of handicapped children in integrated settings do not clearly show such advantages. Others question the law because they fear adverse effects on non-handicapped children who may receive less attention from teachers who are preoccupied with a few special children in the class. Simple prejudice directed toward those who are "different" probably accounts for the resistance of others. In part, the controversy reflects differences of opinion between conservatives and liberals in and out of education.

Efforts have already been made to have this law, passed in 1972, repealed. Administrators in schools are unsure of their responsibility and uncertain of the best method of implementing the law. One problem is that the law was mandated to go into effect in September of 1974. It might have been easier to implement something like the new Arkansas law which provides for more gradual implementation.

Seeking redress or service though administrative changes and legislation can be futile; many professionals in the field urge that court actions be instituted only after other resources are exhausted.

Meanwhile, many professional organizations have attempted to sway their members and use their prestige to aid others in getting new legislation as well as adding provisions to both new and old legislation. This approach is exemplified by the recently published position paper on "The Right to Habilitation of Persons Who are Mentally Retarded" which was published by the American Association on Mental Deficiency. Concerning an individual's right to service, the paper includes the following:

> Among the service rights specifically recognized by the Association are:
>
> (a)   The right to a free public education appropriate to the individual's needs;
>
> (c)   The right, in accordance with a written, individualized program plan, to such training, rehabilitation, habilitation, therapeutic and counseling services as will assist the individual to develop to his or her maximal potential;

In developing that statement one committee member suggested that the child should also have the right to attend the school of his choice. When it was pointed out that such a "right" could be contrary to federal court rulings such as the famed decision of Judge Garrity in Boston, no more was heard of the suggestion. Nevertheless, the rights of handicapped persons and parents of handicapped children to participate in educational planning seems to be a forward step.

The right to education movement and the suits have been based in constitutional law. Most of the special educators who have supplied data and information for those entering suits are persons of high respectability and great wisdom. A few vociferous persons, however, have made much of the constitutional right to "life, liberty and the pursuit of happiness," apparently unaware that the Declaration of Independence and the Constitution differ as to what is a legal right. Some of these partially informed individuals, as well as others with more reason for their opinions, will doubtless continue to fight for educational provisions for disabled children. As long as appropriate provisions are made, maybe it makes little difference who fights. It will matter, however, if the best possible provisions are not made. It will matter even more if we fail, as we so often have, to try and determine the effectiveness of programs provided. Millions of children were placed in special classes and hundreds of millions of dollars were spent before loud voices cried out for assessment of those classes. It is to be anticipated that the future will require new or different programs. Let us assume that special educators recognize that, and will try to provide evidence of the degree to which provisions currently in use are helpful, lest some over-taxed citizens try to revoke the right to education for handicapped children and make the issue hot again.

Mainstreaming and Normalization

In the late sixties, a new word was added to the American vocabulary...or at least a new definition. From a northern European language, the work *normaliserrad* was translated into *NORMAL-IZATION* in English. And it arrived in capitals. In 1969 Bank-Mikkelsen defined normalization as letting the mentally retarded obtain an existence as close to normal as possible. That same year, Bengt Nirje commented that normalization means a normal rhythm of the day, implies a normal routine of life, and a normal rhythm of the year with holidays. It also assumes an opportunity to undergo normal developmental experiences in the life cycle, consideration for the choices and wishes and desires of the handicapped person, and living in a bisexual world. These principles and approaches have attained wide acceptance among many special education leaders in this country. Having their start in the area of mental retardation, they have been applied to the deaf, the blind, the mentally ill, to all the handicapped. Normalization has been hailed and has also caused consternation, resistance, and deep concern.

These concerns reflect not only our reluctance to make changes, but a very real fear that some individuals in need of protection may not be able to get such protection any more. One of the beliefs of the normalization group is that handicapped persons have the right to take risks. The other side questions how much risk is acceptable, especially for persons who have needed protection in the past. Numerous "horror" stories of persons whose welfare was greatly compromised by the over-zealous application of what is a parody of the normalization principle are well known: Former institution residents who managed to get into stressful situations between after-care visits of the case worker ended on skid row. Children were placed in foster homes which "blew-up." Mass impregnation resulted when young ladies were placed in community living situations before getting education about some aspects of the community they did not know about. These are failures of normalization that everyone wishes to avoid. Such failures are used to emphasize the failure of the principle. It might be more appropriate to see them as failures in preparation or in understanding the true meaning of normalization as set forth by Bank-Mikkelsen. The term itself is now taboo in some settings. Perhaps the issue can get some resolution after the first controversies die down and special educators recognize the normalization does not mean making handicapped persons normal, but simply provides those aspects of normal existence that they can enjoy, participate in, contribute to.

Mainstreaming is the public school equivalent of normalization. There have been numerous attacks on public schools for segregating too many children, particularly minority group children, for such groups have been over-represented in special classes. Little has been said about too many children in speech correction programs, in classes for partially sighted, in pre-school programs; instead, debates have centered around segregated classes for retarded or disturbed children. But the public schools, and particularly special educators and school psychologists, have been criticized for placements of "too many" minority group children in special classes for the retarded. No doubt some of the criticism is justified. Much is not. Many have pressed in vain for facilities other than special classes. Many have requested a budget which would provide for more remedial reading teachers, more bilingual programs, more ancillary services. For years, the special educator or school psychologist was faced with the problem of having a child in need of special services, but having a very limited range of special services available. With new legislation for bilingual education and a greater range of provisions, some of the furor may die down. We need to remember, though, that the majority of children with special needs have received no special services through the system itself. Thousands of dedicated teachers have worked overtime, taken special courses on handicapped children at their own expense, and sought the advice of specialists in order to provide for special needs children in their regular classes.

It is simply not true that handicapped children have received "nothing" as is so often stated. The problem is that they have not been recognized or provided for in formal arrangements made by the system. Even the most dedicated regular class teachers have not been able to give many of these children the attention they needed. So, we arrived at mainstreaming. Mainstreaming means that insofar as possible the handicapped student will be served in the regular class and regular school. As noted, most of them always have been served there, but not with carefully planned special services. With mainstreaming, special education programming is integrated with the rest of the program and the child stays with non-handicapped children.

Mainstreaming is the approach of the seventies. Many special educators and some other educators think it is a great move forward. Others disagree, as did one regular class teacher who quipped: "Oh, ho! Now we got pollution in the mainstream!" That remark tells as much about the attitude of the teacher toward handicapped children as it does about her wit. We cannot deny, however, that some of our efforts to mainstream have been less than successful. Nor have we always made an effort to determine the results of mainstreaming. A few studies are beginning to suggest that in the decades since the sociometric studies of Orville Johnson and Samuel Kirk and Willie Kate Baldwin, little has changed with regard to the willingness of "normal" children to make friends with handicapped children in regular classes. What is our responsibility? How can we change attitudes of teachers and pupils? It is much harder than changing classrooms.

Labels and Classification

Much effort has recently been directed toward the eradication of labels within the field of special education. The special education law in Massachusetts (Chapter 766 of the General Laws of 1972) requires that the term "special needs child" be substituted for the more familiar terms of educable mentally retarded, emotionally disturbed, etc. The *New England Journal of Medicine* has just recently provided an orientation to the law for its readers; one of the summary remarks of that article states, "The law discourages the diagnostic labeling of children, thereby avoiding the risk of self-fulfilling prophecy."

Obviously, very responsible people have been greatly influenced by such statements as that which Rosenthal and Jacobson made in *Pygmalion in the Classroom* (1968), "The evidence presented...suggests rather strongly that children who are expected by their teachers to gain intellectually in fact do show greater intellectual gains after one year than do children of whom such gains are not expected." The devastating criticisms of Rosenthal and Jacobson's work did not seem to weaken the effects of the conclusions reached by the authors of *Pygmalion*. But, post-Pygmalion researchers have found no significant influence of teacher expectancy on the variables they studied. In our own earlier research (Spielberg, 1973), we found that the effects of teacher expectations are more complex and subtle than Rosenthal and Jacobson's work suggested. We found that although labeling a child may stimulate certain expectation statements made about the child, those expectations are not necessarily translated into behavior which affects learning. Even more important, expectations were found to be fluid and unstable. Our data indicated that teachers significantly changed their expectation statements within 15 minutes of interacting with a child. Thus, teachers were not for any appreciable amount of time unduly influenced by the effects of labeling.

The furor over labels is perhaps the hottest of all and it is probably the one on which there is the greatest agreement among special educators. Labels are bad, period. No exceptions. I do not agree with the majority. Sometimes it is possible to get second thoughts in some of the less vociferous persons who decry labels by asking whether they would object so strongly to having the label of *gifted* or *talented* (or even *men* or *beautiful*) placed on them. We are too often confusing the label with the human tendency to expect too much of a label. We use the term *label* instead of the word *classification* (just as we say *education of the public* rather than *propaganda)*. A label is simply a term from a classification system that denotes the group into which one falls.

As Clements and Warren noted in 1975:

> Classification is simply a scientific procedure for systematic arrangement of individuals, units, or events into groups in which the individuals of the group share one

or more common denominators. The use of a clsssification system should lead to the development of schematic sets of factors which are characteristic of the group within the system. Such an approach can provide a base for obtaining precise information about the nature, prevention, and amelioration of (associated conditions).

No objections can be raised to trying to obtain precise information about the nature, prevention, and amelioration of a handicap. The fault lies not in the label but in those who misuse it; no amount of effort to develop new verbal sands in which to bury our heads will change the human proclivity to over-generalize, to disparage that which is considered unacceptable, to denigrate the different individual. We are tilling the wrong field when we say labels are at fault; what is needed is an effort to get others to recognize that it is all right to be different sometimes, that disabled persons have contributions to make, that the American way is to provide for *all* and not just for those who are in the majority.

The 1975 Hobbs report has noted that:

> Classification can profoundly affect what happens to a child. It can open doors to services and experiences that child needs to grow in competence, to become a person sure of his worth and appreciative of the worth of others, to live with zest, and to know joy. On the other hand classification...can blight the life of a child, reduce opportunity, diminish his competence and self esteem, alienate him from others, nurture a meanness of spirit, and make him less of a person than he could become. Nothing less than the futures of children is at stake.

I agree that the futures of children are at stake. I submit that it is not classification which makes the difference, but the fact that we so often stereotype and denigrate, and deny others on the basis of classification.

It is simply not the case that labels are always and all bad, even labels which suggest that a person is less complete than others in society. There are data which strongly suggest that when a child is given a label, others may think more kindly of him, may be more likely to expect of him performance within his capacity, may value him more than if he had the same problem but did not have the label. In our own work we have found that whether a child is labeled or described without the label, the same kinds of statements are made about him. If this finding is replicated, I would submit that the issue of whether to classify or label a child is not the issue. The issue is whether we can accept other human beings as worthy even when they may look different, have less to contribute to society, or even be a burden on some of us.

Early Identification

This issue also enjoys a favorable majority opinion. But there are some who are deeply concerned. There has been a great deal of new work with some of the rare disorders associated with deafness, blindness, and mental retardation. Now it is possible to identify early in life several of the metabolic disorders associated with later handicap. For example, Robert Guthrie has a simple blood test; from samples of blood taken in the first few days of life he can identify about a dozen serious disorders. For some of these disorders, treatments are available which can prevent later damage to the child. For these rare disorders, failure to provide early identification would be a crime. (Nevertheless, some professionals and many laymen are opposed to using Guthrie's test for sickle cell anemia because it is most often found in a minority group and is thus "stigmatizing.") There are techniques such as Lyle Lloyd's TROCA for identifying children with hearing deficits at an early age. For these problems, early identification can be extremely important.

Thus, we have moved into a stage where early identification of all kinds of problems is promoted. There is federal legislation which requires states to screen for disabilities early in life. States, with rare exceptions, have not complied. There are professionals of good repute who are strongly opposed to early screening. In part, this is a part of the anti-labeling movement. More often, it reflects a deep concern that children may fail to get the kinds of service they need and may even be stigmatized early in life. They may be over-protected by their mothers. Perhaps a greater danger lies in the degree of human suffering of parents and children when they face the "fact" that the child is "learning disabled," or when they are told that the child is "emotionally disturbed;" the problem arises from the fact that good identification of some handicaps is difficult to achieve.

This is so for several reasons. Young children vary widely in their rates of development. A child may seem "slow" at an early age, but show a growth spurt shortly thereafter. Young children are difficult to test because they have not learned to cooperate in the types of situations demanded by formal testing. The differences between normal and handicapped children may be much less obvious in early childhood than in later years because the slow child's deficits become cumulative and more obvious as he grows older. It is difficult to clearly identify emotional disturbance in early years for many children because it is not uncommon for normal young children to behave much in the manner of older children with emotional disturbances. Thus, the essential question revolves around selection of those disabilities which must be and can be identified early in life, rather than wholesale efforts to identify every possible problem which might be serious at some later date.

Assessments and Uses of Tests

As early as 1927 the problem of misuse of tests was noted by

Morgan and Gilliland in *An Introduction to Psychology:*

> It is a mistake to apply such names as *idiot, imbecile, moron,* or *genius* on the basis of a single mental test. The test must be backed up by other findings. We cannot stress this statement too much. Much harm has been done by giving a child a name implying that he was feeble-minded, merely because he did not pass a test given by some novice...It must not be assumed that an intelligence test quotient even when carefully determined tells all about a child's mental ability. Sometimes a child with an intelligence quotient of .70 or .80 may do very satisfactory school work and show no signs of dullness while some with high intelligence quotients may seem very dull. Application, persistence, and zeal sometimes make up for slowness in ability, and laziness may counteract the ability of the superior child.
>
> ...Despite the fact that millions of school children have been given mental tests, too little correct use has been made of the results. Teachers and others have given tests and have assumed that there was some virtue attached in doing so, letting the matter rest there...On the other hand, some are too eager in their zeal for mental tasks and have failed to realize that the things that these tests measure are only one factor in school and in life outside the school. Some have tried to explain too much on the basis of mental test scores. Some have shown a tendency to brand the child and use this as an excuse for neglect. On the other hand, the real value of these tests should not be slighted because of some unfortunate attempts to try to make too great or improper use of the test scores (pp. 297-300).

In 1941, David Wechsler was aware of the problems and wrote:

> There has been much discussion, pro and con, of this question, most of which, in our opinion, is not very conclusive. In the end it resolves itself into a very practical problem, to wit: whether or not psychometric tests alone can be used for classifying an individual as a mental defective. On this point there cannot be much dispute; the answer is definitely "No." Accumulated experience has shown that in spite of the great value of psychometric tests in detecting and measuring mental deficiency, they cannot be used as an exclusive criterion of it. It is not possible to define any but the lowest grades of mental deficiency in terms of mental age or IQ alone. This is shown on the one hand by the fact that there are many individuals with IQ's considerably higher than those which are ordinarily set as the upper limits of mental deficiency but who nevertheless show themselves as definitely defective in their behavior. On the other hand, there are individuals with IQ's or mental ages considerably below those set as the limits or normality whose entire life history is that of a non-defective individual.
>
> ...The difficulty of making differential diagnoses in certain cases does not, however, justify the failure to differentiate them altogether, much less the persistence of a practice which assumes that mental deficiency can be diagnosed through a single approach (pp. 51-54).

It would be difficult to improve on the comments made by those writers more than three decades ago. There has been great controversy over the use of intelligence tests. Most of it might have been less bitter if the words of those who designed the tests had been heeded. We live now in a situation where some school systems have "outlawed" intelligence tests, at least for the time being. This leaves the schools in a position of having to use clinical judgments, perhaps supplemented by criterion-referenced tests and teacher-made tests. These are useful devices, but they cannot give the kind of relative and comparative data needed to make sound decisions, at least according to some professionals. Trying to guess whether a child is learning as well as he can when one only knows what he is doing makes the job a difficult one. Some writers have suggested using clinical judgment to estimate intellectual functioning. When working with profoundly retarded children this seems reasonable to most professionals. Failure to use reliable measures for more difficult decision-making seems foolish, especially when much clinical judgment is like trying to measure a balloon with a rubber tape measure.

Some of those who propose that intelligence tests should be used (by well trained and well informed personnel, of course) argue that any information which gives a better understanding of a child should be used. They point out that the development of norms for minority populations is probably a useful device because it can indicate how a child stands relative to others with similar backgrounds. However, they point out that the child will still probably have to cope with the general culture as well as his own sub-culture and thus it is useful to have an indication about his functioning as compared with the general population. They also attack the use of "Spanish language" versions of tests, because the Puerto Rican child's Spanish is not the same as that of the Mexican-American's, much less that of the child from Madrid. One would expect that the efforts of Jane Mercer in California may give us better insight into this situation when her norms for minority group children are in use for a few years. Meanwhile, the debates will no doubt continue for a few years, as some psychologists use tests and others do not.

There has been less criticism of tests other than intelligence tests, except for the campaign against projective personality measures a few years ago. The personality test battle has since abated. Group tests of personality are not used with handicapped children very often. Most of the personality work is now done by clinical psychologists working either in clinics or in schools, but special educators are not often involved in such work at this time. Other tests in wide use are perhaps less controversial. There are a very large number in use, most of them providing norms for the general population. But, when one looks carefully at the standardization sample (e.g., 900 children in a single school district used as "representative" of the total population), one cannot but wonder why they have not been more controversial. When one sees several tests which are assumed to measure the same ability given to a child with very different results coming out, one wonders again.

Measurement instruments by the dozen have appeared and are widely used in special education. Some of them are very helpful and some are not. At this time, caution is urged by those who train special educators. This area is likely to become a battleground again if those interested in test development and validation do not begin an intensive study of the usefulness of the many tests of perceptual-motor skills, socialization skills, visual-motor intregration, personality characteristics, and specific achievements. Fortunately, the recent literature suggests that the tests are being subjected to rigid scrutiny by investigators. It may be that better measures may be developed without too great a controversy, or at least not so great as that besetting intelligence tests at this time.

Techniques of Instruction

Open classrooms for the severely retarded? Behavior modification for the deaf? One-on-one teaching for the learning disabled? Use of "peer tutors"? Volunteers? Creative classrooms? Token economy or engineered classes? TA for the pre-school blind? Montessori?

As in education all over the country, there are debates about how what should be taught. The debates may be characterized as being between the structured and the unstructured adherents, with various schools of thought falling between.

Handicapped children pose many great problems to special educators; if they did not, these children would not need special education. Most of them are very difficult to teach. Thus, when only small gains occur, teachers are apt to embrace any new promising technique. Some have taken the more psychodynamic approach of emphasizing self-expression and creativity. Others have sought the security of small gains through the use of applied analysis of behavior, or behavior modification. Unusually bitter arguments have surrounded the use of behavior modification techniques in classrooms, as well as outside them. These arguments seem surprising when one reviews the definition of the procedure as used by those who developed it: Sidney Bijou, Leonard Krasner, Teodoro Ayllon, Montrose Wolf, for example. Behavior modification simply means using the methods and experimental findings of psychologists in a systematic manner with the aim of altering behaviors. The principles and procedures are intended to increase, restrict, teach, maintain, or reduce behaviors. These are the aims of all who teach. Methods include positive or negative reinforcement to increase behaviors (roughly analogous to rewards), systematic planning for step-by-step development of a behavior through shaping (similar to lesson-planning and curriculum design), and continuous monitoring of changes in behavior through objective observations and in quantifiable ways (evaluation). Perhaps the use of punishment in some instances has led to much of the controversy, but punishment in training children is no new technique.

There is little doubt that behavior modification is useful for certain types of handicapped children learning certain skills. The application of established psychological principles to the acquisition and maintenance of certain behaviors cannot be denied. The procedures are especially useful in developing self-help skills, academic materials which can be quantified (e.g., addition, word recognition) and some social skills. There is less evidence that these procedures are easy to use in developing reasoning skills, complex social interactions, abstractions. Many of the critics of the behavior modifiers point to the danger of controlling other persons. But all teachers, as well as parents and society in general, try to control the behaviors of others. When teachers persuade children to sit in classes, turn in written work, paint a mural, or tie shoes they are attempting to control behavior. The difference seems to be that the behavior modifiers have reported some spectacular successes with some behaviors and thus raised the possibility of total control.

The present state of the science strongly suggests that it is not likely that there will be any behavior modifiers with sufficient skill to make permanent robots out of children. The techniques are still in their infancy and human behavior is extremely complex. Nevertheless, it is an area of some danger because one could more easily succeed with behavior modification than with other techniques if one chose to keep children silent, obedient, and in check. This is particularly true for retarded children who have less ability to outwit the teacher. (I must admit, however, that I have seen children with IQ's below 30 keep an entire professional staff in line, thus proving that some children learn to be excellent "behavior modifiers".)

On the other side, the behavior modification contingent sometimes accuses others of being soft, too emotional, too concerned with feelings and not enough concerned with helping the child learn those skills he desperately needs to cope with a world made very difficult for a handicapped child.

Both groups have worthwhile points to make. Some of the things a child needs to learn cannot be taught by behavior modification, as the outstanding professionals in the field such as Sidney Bijou freely admit. Bijou remarks that no sensible teacher would set up a token economy classroom for children learning well without it. Some tasks can be learned more efficiently by using behavior modification. Someday, perhaps both sides will recognize that much of what each side is doing goes back to Thorndike's law of effect, which stated over half a century ago that those behaviors which are followed by pleasant consequences are more likely to be repeated (other things being equal) when a similar situation arises.

Summary

There are a number of very important issues in special education in the seventies. Most of them are not new. As early as 1909 a teacher presented at a national meeting a paper that discussed the problems of special classes, including stigma, and later effects of "special" treatments. She even hinted at the right to education. The debates seem to be cyclic, the weight of opinion being in one direction at one time and swinging to another direction later. In part, these issues reflect changes in education generally. They also reflect the social scene. In many cases, there are value judgments involved. How the issues will be resolved, if they ever are, cannot be predicted. What can be predicted is that as long as there are children whose physical, intellectual, or cultural endowments are insufficient to provide the child with easy access to those skills needed to cope with an increasingly difficult society, there will be need for special educators to aid those with problems. Whether the helpers will be called special educators or something else is not vital. They will be giving special help to special individuals; work that is vital, and work that must transcend ephemeral issues and purposeless debate.

REFERENCES

Claiborn, W. L. "Expectancy Effects in the Classroom: A Failure to Replicate." *Journal of Educational Psychology,* 1969, 60, pp. 377-383.

Clements, J. D. and Warren, S. A. "Preface to a Preface." *Mental Retardation,* 13, 3, pp. 2-3.

Fleming, E. S. and Anttonen, R. G. "Teacher Expectancy or My Fair Lady." *American Educational Research Journal,* 1971, 8, pp. 241-252.

Grossman, H. J., Warren, S. A., Begab, M. J., Eyman, R., Nihira, K., and O'Connor, G. *Manual on Terminology and Classification in Mental Retardation,* Washington: American Association on Mental Deficiency, 1973.

Hobbs, N. J. *The Futures of Children,* Nashville: Vanderbilt University, 1975.

Massachusetts Acts and Resolves, Chapter 766, An Act Further Regulating Programs for Children Requiring Special Education and Providing Reimbursement Therefor.

Morgan, J. J. B. and Gilliland, A. R. *An Introduction to Psychology,* 1927, New York: Macmillan Co.

New England Journal of Medicine, May 15, 1975.

Rosenthal, R. and Jacobson, L. *Pygmalion in the Classroom: Teacher Expectation and Pupil's Intellectual Development,* New York: Holt, Rinehart, and Winston, 1968.

Spielberg, D. B. "Labeling, Teacher Expectations, Pupil Intelligence Level, and Conditions of Learning." *Dissertation Abstracts International,* 1973.

Thorndike, R. L. "Pygmalion in the Classroom." *American Educational Research Journal, review of R. Rosenthal and L. Jacobson.* 1967, , n p. 708-711.

Wachs, T. D. "Personality Testing of the Handicapped: A Review." *Journal of Projective Techniques and Personality Assessment,* 1966, 30, pp. 339-355.

Warren, S. A. "Psychological Evaluation of the Mentally Retarded." H. J. Grossman (Ed.). *Mental Retardation,* Pediatric Clinics of North America, 1968.

Wechsler, D. *The Measurement of Adult Intelligence,* 2nd Edition, Baltimore: William and Wilkins Co., 1941.

VIII.

BILINGUAL EDUCATION

By Maria Estela Brisk

American schools are not, for the first time, confronting the challenge of bilingual education. Non-English speaking settlers in the eighteenth and nineteenth centuries propagated their own languages in public as well as private and parochial schools. Massive immigration in the late nineteenth and early twentieth centuries added bilingual aspirations of new citizens until, as a reaction against the languages and religions of the newer minorities, the English-speaking majority of Americans assured passage of laws requiring the use of English in public schools. By 1920 laws in a majority of states required the use of English as a medium of instruction at all levels of public education.

This assimilationist position is crumbling. Intensified migration of Spanish speakers from the Caribbean and Latin America, resurgence of ethnic identity, especially among American Indians and Asians, and the recognition that primary and secondary education has regressed in many urban and rural settings due to language difficulties have forced federal, state, and even local education authorities to revive bilingual education. Title VII ("The Bilingual Education Act") of the Elementary and Secondary Education Amendments of 1968 gave the movement for bilingual education a national character. At least 18 states have passed or introduced legislation requiring bilingual instruction.

A number of law suits brought in recent years, mostly by parents of bilingual children, against school districts maintaining unjust educational practices are an important element in the trend to provide bilingual children with an adequate education. Most recently the Office of Civil Rights has issued guidelines for schools to comply with the 1974 Supreme Court decision in the case of *Lau vs. Nichols*. This decision requires school districts to provide equal educational opportunities for students whose primary or home language is other than English.

In 1973 there were nearly 400 bilingual programs operating in 36 states, the District of Columbia, Guam, Puerto Rico, the Trust Territories, and the Virgin Islands. Program support came from a variety of federal, state, local, and private sources.

Unfortunately, even the term "bilingual education" connotes different meanings to different people. It has been applied to foreign language teaching, to teaching English to non-English speakers, or to the use of two languages as mediums of instruction. Neither "foreign" language training nor teaching English to non-native speakers represent "bilingual" education. Teaching a foreign language a few times a week does not produce bilinguals. Offering English instruction to a non-native speaker without providing instruction in his own language at the same time will cause, in the case of children, loss of fluency in the native language.

Nature of Languages

In the United States, of course, English is always one of the languages used in bilingual education. Programs presently under way use 32 different languages: 19 American Indian and Eskimo, 7 Indo-European, 5 languages of the Pacific Islands, and an Asian language. (See Figure 2.) The nature of these languages differs. The differences have an effect on the structure and implementation of the bilingual program.

English is a national and world language, used widely in social communication, education, work, technology, and other situations. It is also a written language with extensive literature. Spanish, French, the rest of the Indo-European languages, and Chinese also have a long tradition of use in education. Each has a technological vocabulary, is widely used in commerce, and has a substantial literature. Languages of the American Indians, Eskimos, and Pacific Island communities are considered local vernaculars—used in a limited area by a limited number of speakers. Some of these languages lack written systems. Written materials among those with alphabets are still scarce. They lack technological vocabulary. All languages have the power to adapt to new situations, but it involves an enormous effort to introduce new vocabulary and produce written materials.

FIGURE 2. BILINGUAL EDUCATION PROGRAMS IN THE U.S.A.

Languages	No. Programs
I. American Indian and Eskimo (8 percent of total)	**31**
1. Athabascan (AK)*	1
2. Cherokee (OK)	1
3. Cheyenne (MT)	1
4. Choctaw (OK)	1
5. Cree (MT)	1
6. Crow (MT)	2
7. Inupiat Eskimo (AK)	1
8. Keres (NM)	3
9. Lakota (SD)	1
10. Miccosukee (FL)	1
11. Navajo (AR, CO, NM, UT)	8
12. Papago (AR)	1
13. Passamaquoddy (ME)	1
14. Pomo (CA)	1
15. Seminole (OK)	1
16. Tewa (NM)	1
17. Ute (CO)	1
18. Yupik Eskimo (AK)	3
19. Zuni (NM)	1
II. Chinese (CA, MA, NY) (1.6 percent of total)	**6**

Languages	No. Programs
III. Indo-European Languages (88.8 per cent of total)	**344**
1. French (CA, DC, LA, MA, ME, MI, NH, NY, VT)	18
2. German (MD)	1
3. Greek (CT, MA)	4
4. Italian (CT, MA)	9
5. Portuguese (CA, CT, MA, RI)	21
6. Russian (OR)	1
7. Spanish (AR, CA, CO, CT, DE, DC, FL, ID, IL, IN, KS, LA, MA, MI, MN, MS, MT, NJ, NM, NY, ND, OH, OR, PA, PR, RI, TN, TX, UT, V. ISL., WA, WI)	290
IV. Languages of the Pacific Islands (1.6 percent of total)	**6**
1. Chamorro (GUAM, TR. TERR.)	2
2. Palauan (TR. TERR.)	1
3. Ponapean (TR. TERR.)	1
4. Tagalog (CA)	1
5. Yapese (TR. TERR.)	1
Total	**387**

SOURCE: Maria Estela Brisk, *Directory of Bilingual Education Programs: 1972-1974* (Center for Applied Linguistics, 1973), Appendix II.

*Indicates the name of the state where the programs are found.

Dialects

A language develops and changes due to a number of factors peculiar to each region where the language is spoken. Consequently, a language branches into dialects which differ from each other in sound, grammar, and vocabulary. The word *dialect* has a negative connotation for many people. They feel it is an incorrect form of the "standard" language—defined as "the form of a language accepted by and serving as a model to a large speech community"—and which is considered the "correct" form. Not many linguists would adhere to this position. Dialects have a structure of their own. The so-called "mistakes" are used systematically, meaning that they are part of a system of communication that everybody in that speech community uses and understands. All the features of the dialect, then, are "correct" in terms of that dialect. The "standard" is just another form of the language with its own features.

A number of children in this country enter school speaking a dialect of their ethnic language. Puerto Ricans, Cubans, and Mexican-Americans speak different dialects of Spanish. French from Louisiana differs from that spoken in Vermont. Moreover, minority groups have developed their own English dialects—Red English, Chicano English, and so on—structured according to patterns of their ethnic language. Thus, speakers of Chicano English follow an inclination towards usage that parallels Spanish. They choose with more frequency *sofa* and *plate,* rather than *couch* and *dish,* for instance. In Isleta English (spoken by Pueblo Indians in the Rio Grande valley of New Mexico) the use of single and double negation alternate following the structure and meaning found in the Tiwa language. When an Isleta indian says, "He was *never* hurt by *no* ants," he is not making an "error" but is using a systematic pattern with its own meaning.

Most teachers are trained to use the "standard" language. This difference in the form of language between teacher and students can lead to lack of communication and an interference with substantive education. Teachers from the same ethnic group as the children will help bridge this gap, because they may be able to understand and speak the dialect of the children. Unfortunately even some ethnic teachers react negatively to the dialect spoken by their own ethnic group and assume an attitude of correcting a substandard language form. Consequently, the study of dialects should be a major consideration in teacher-training.

The bilingual program has to decide what form of the language will be used for insruction. If the program's purpose is to facilitate instruction in a language the children do not know, the use of a "standard" form can have the same negative effects as the use of a foreign language. In turn, if the "standard" form is the one used in written materials, higher education and employment, children will need to learn it. In a well-conceived program the children will become not only bilingual, but bidialectical.

Objectives

Planners of bilingual education programs pursue distinct goals. Although, as we shall see, the goals are not always explicit or mandated by existing legislation. Some are intended to ease the transition of children who are native speakers of another language into an English language school system. This goal is reflected in the Massachusetts Transitional Bilingual Education Law:

> ...a compensatory program of transitional bilingual education [to] meet the needs of these children [who come from environments where the primary language is other than

English] and facilitate their integration into the regular public school curriculum (Annotated Laws of Massachusetts, p. 40).

Other programs aim at producing functional bilinguals, children able to use and maintain both English and their ethnic language. The language skills of such children determine more specific objectives: to maintain parity of proficiency if children already enjoy bilingual skills, to develop parity if children are essentially monolingual in their ethnic language, or to reviatlize the ethnic language when children customarily use English but the community expects greater ethnic language proficiency. Revitalization is the goal especially among younger generations who have lost their parents to enter into English-speaking society. The National Bilingual Education Law provides grants for all the above goals except for reviatlization. The grants are expected:

to develop and carry out new and imaginative elementary and secondary school programs designed to meet these special educational needs (of children of limited English-speaking ability). (Hearing before the Committee on Education and Labor, p. 76).

So far, native speakers of English who happen to be Eskimos, American Indian, Spanish, and others have been able to participate in bilingual programs because the criteria for classification as a non-English speaker has been either surname or the native language of the parent, rather than the actual language ability of the child. Unfortunately, ignoring the language ability of the children can lead to ineffective teaching and preparation of materials.

Coverage

Bilingual programs differ greatly with respect to who is participating in the program. In a bilingual school the entire curriculum may be bilingual, including in the program all the children in the school regardless of language ability or ethnic affiliation. In other cases the bilingual program complements the regular school curriculum and is geared to the non-English speakers. The degree to which the school commits itself to broad bilingual education largely depends on the number of bilingual children, the availability of funds and personnel, the number of languages—other than English—and political pressures. A program directed only to a particular ethnic group serves only half its purpose. One of the benefits of bilingual education provides the children of the majority knowledge and understanding of the language and culture of groups which are an important part of our pluralistic society. Improving the attitude of the majority will increase self-esteem among minority children, a step forward in the education process of these children.

The number of grades covered will depend on the objective of the program and the availability of funds, materials, and personnel. Most transitional programs limit the bilingual instruction to three years.

Because of the great demand and the lack of funds, materials and qualified teachers, the non-transitional programs usually start at the lowest grade and add one grade every year with the goal of making the whole school bilingual. There are some drawbacks in this system. The children in the upper grades do not profit from bilingual education since the effective use of the two languages is enhanced when the whole school is participating. The faculty and staff in the regular school may feel threatened by the bilingual program and may prove reluctant to cooperate. Ideally the entire school should be converted to a bilingual curriculum.

Curriculum

There are a variety of approaches for confronting each of the two major curricular issues in bilingual education: language training, and the medium of instruction for other subjects. Language training is generally approached in two ways—for the native speaker and for the non-native speaker. This distinction is made because of their different language-learning needs. Reading is taught first in the dominant language. Reading in the second language is postponed until a certain degree of oral fluency is attained. Most research supports this approach, but the St. Lambert Experiment successfully employed a completely different technique. By "total immersion" in the second language, the children acquired remarkable oral fluency and reading ability in the second language and transferred the reading skills to the first language. Without any instruction they were able to read in their first language. This experiment is described more thoroughly on page 106.

Both languages are used as mediums of instruction in a conventional bilingual program. The choice of subjects to be taught in each language will depend on the nature of the language, the use of each language, and the availability of teachers and materials. There are a number of other decisions to be made related to the curriculum such as time allotted for each language, classroom arrangements, strategies used to teach in two languages and the role of teachers and aides. The most common pattern is to have parallel curricula; teaching language arts, a language as a second language, and other subjects in both languages. The children are separated for language instruction while they are together for other subjects which are taught bilingually or in alternated days for each language.

Analysis of Three Bilingual Educational Schools

As enumerated above, there are a large number of factors to be considered in planning a bilingual program. No research has controlled all of these factors to show what "works." A closer look at three successful and very different programs may indicate some of the characteristics that make a bilingual program succeed.

Coral Way School, in Coral Way, Florida, is an elementary Spanish-English bilingual school founded in 1963 by middle-class Cuban refugees anxious for their children to preserve their language and culture. The school started with about the same number of Spanish and English speakers. The curriculum was repeated in each language—one in the morning, the other in the afternoon. All the children followed the curriculum in both languages. They were separated in the early grades by language proficiency and grouped together in the upper grades. Evaluations of the program indicated high achievement. In the upper grades a high degree of bilingualism among both groups of students was achieved. Lately, the student body has changed and the methods have become less successful. A number of the Cuban children entering the school are bilingual or have English as their dominant language. The Anglo population has diminished while a number of poorer Spanish speakers have enrolled.

It is hard to determine specifically what it is that is not working. One can speculate, however, that lower class bilingual children have problems and needs that are not exclusively linguistic in nature. These children often come from rural communities and settle in a crowded urban ghetto. Their parents have a poor education, do not know the language, and in general find it very difficult to offer the support needed by the children in this new setting.

The John F. Kennedy School is a bilingual German-English elementary and secondary school started by a group of private German and American citizens in Berlin in 1960. It presently serves over 2000 students: 50 percent German, 40 percent Americans and 10 percent of other nationalities. The curriculum is taught bilingually except language instruction which is given in the student's native language. Students are regrouped according to level of proficiency for instruction in their second language. Reading and writing in the second language does not start until the second year in school. The alternation of languages in the other classes depends on the teacher, students and materials. All teachers are bilingual and most students become bilingual after a few years. American and German students, parents, and teachers are strongly encouraged to mix in formal and informal situations. An interesting attitude observed is the bilingual student's willingness to help the monolingual.

Achievement in mathematics, social studies and other academic subjects is comparable to that of monolingual children. Achievement in each language, when considered separately, is less than that observed in monolingual speakers of each language. But considering achievement in both languages as a whole, the development of the Kennedy School children is superior to monolinguals. For instance, the number of English lexical items known by the bilingual child can be less than that of a monolingual child of the same age, but the total number of English and German lexical items known far surpasses that of a monolingual child. Most children, especially the Germans who stay throughout the 13 years of school, achieve native proficiency in the second language. The program has also encouraged bilingualism among parents and has developed among the children a respect for other native languages.

The St. Lambert Experiment was planned by a group of middle-class, many professional, parents who wanted to find out what would happen if their English-speaking children received instruction in French. The program started in an English school in Montreal in 1965 with a kindergarten pilot project. It has presently reached the junior high school level. The entire curriculum is in French through kindergarten and first grade. English language arts is introduced in second grade while the rest of the teaching continues in French. English instruction increases up to about 40 percent in the upper grades. An evaluation done after the fifth year shows that the children retain native English-speaking ability; there is no cognitive retardation. While they do not acquire native proficiency in French they use it with a much greater degree of fluency than children who have learned French with the traditional French-as-a-Second-Language approach. Lambert and Tucker conclude that:

> There is no question that given opportunities to use French in diverse social situations, the Experiment children, and others following them in the program, could become indistinguishable from native speakers of French in their oral expression...(Lambert and Tucker, p.152).

Instruction in Puerto Rico provides an example of how second language fluency is not achieved when the language is not used outside the classroom. English was the language of instruction used by Puerto Rico during the first half of this century, yet Spanish remained as the population's strongest language. Achievement in English was not always high.

There are some important features common to all three programs. First, they were successful in educating children to become bilingual. Second, the results of the evaluations on the same group of children improved with time. This is true of most programs. Third, they were initiated by the community and continue to receive great support from it. These three programs are not representative of most situations in the United States, where most of the bilingual schools are found in poor city neighborhoods or in small rural towns. The children attending the three schools described in this paper come from middle-class families, with well-educated parents and did not suffer social discrimination.

Of great significance is the experience of lower class minority children in these programs. At Coral Way these children did not perform well. It is likely that the nature of the problems minority children have at school transcend linguistic sensitivity. Comparative evaluations of bilingual schools attended by lower-class children are essential in order to determine how variables such as place of origin, education of parents, social class and others, influence school performance.

Conclusion

Before instituting a bilingual education program those in charge of planning should answer some questions:

(1) Does the program enjoy community support? Parents should be fully informed about the program and about bilingual education in general. Programs imposed on a community generate parental distrust. The tendency to assimilate everyone into the mainstream of "American" life, language, and culture is well established. Any change is seen by some parents as an effort to segregate their children.

(2) Is there an opportunity to use both languages outside the classroom? In order to promote the use of languages—especially those of minorities—outside the classroom, the bilingual school should build positive attitudes towards these languages and their cultures. Extracurricular activities should be planned to bring native speakers of both languages together. Ethnic balance in the school is obviously the ideal situation to achieve this goal.

(3) Has the native language proficiency of the children entering the program been determined? To effectively plan the instruction, an evaluation of the language ability of the children is essential. It should be established on a purely linguistic basis rather than on the ethnic affiliation of the children.

(4) Are the teachers and staff familiar with the dialect and culture of the children? Teachers and staff should learn as much as possible about the dialects and culture of the children in order to understand and establish positive attitudes towards the children's speech and behavior.

(5) What is the best method of instruction to be used? This question remains unanswered due to lack of proper evaluations. Several methods seem to work for middle-class children, as we have illustrated above.

The total immersion method which introduces instruction in the second language only for the first two years of schooling, followed by gradual introduction of the first language is being successfully used in Canada to teach French to native speakers of English. A Spanish speaking student entering a monolingual English program in the U.S.A. finds himself in a comparable situation. He does not, however, in many cases adjust to the situation and continues to drop behind in school achievement. There are two important factors in addition to class difference which should be considered in a comparison between the Canadian and U.S. situations: first, in the case of Canada, the second language French, is that of the minority; in the U.S.A., English, the second language, is that of the dominant population. Second, the non-French speaking child doesn't have to compete with French-speaking children in the same classroom, whereas the Spanish speaking child in the U.S.A. is placed in a class with native English speakers and with a teacher who may not be equipped to help him.

A second method, as in Coral Way and other programs found in private schools throughout the world, repeats the curriculum in both languages the same day. This method, although it has proven successful, is hard to implement on a wide basis due to the number of trained teachers needed.

A third method separates children for language instruction, while other academic subjects are taught bilingually, either by freely alternating the languages in one class, dividing the class time in two and using a different language in each half, or alternating language use everyday. This method is used in a number of programs in the United States. Subject matter teachers who are not completely fluent in both languages should work on a team with native speakers of the other language in order to avoid giving the children a poor model of the second language.

In most cases, methods are chosen for their feasability rather than their effectiveness. In working with the bilingual students in the U.S.A., it is important to consider psychological and sociological, as well as linguistic variables.

In committing itself to bilingual education the schools, the states, and the nation face a dilemma. Communication with parents, teacher-training, preparation of materials, and evaluation of pilot projects representing different methods should precede actual classroom instruction; yet the children could profit from bilingual education right away. In this country the approach has been to start instruction and prepare parents, teachers, materials, and evaluations with the program underway. This policy has not always led to success. Programs still lack trained teachers, materials and evaluations are not always adequate.

After five years of Title VII in operation there is no statement with respect to what seems to work. Consequently, some planning and preparation should precede classroom instruction for better results. In addition, more commitment at the state and local level is needed since Title VII programs only benefit 200,000 of the 5 million children in need of bilingual education.

The emphasis put on culture to enhance the self-esteem and identity of this large segment of the American population is a crucial positive factor of bilingual education. When people do not feel inferior, they can become a productive force in the society, contributing their values, culture, and language.

REFERENCES

Annotated Laws of Massachusetts. Vol. 2-C, Chapter 71A, Supplement, p. 40.

Engle, Patricia. "Language Medium in Early School Years for Minority Language Groups." *Review of Educational Research,* Vol. 45, No. 2, pp. 283-321.

Gumperz, John J. "Types of Linguistic Communities." Joshua Fishman (Ed.), *Readings in the Sociology of Language* The Hague: Mouton, 1968, p. 466.

Hearings before the Committee on Education and Labor. 92nd Congress, 1st Session, 1971, p. 76.

Lambert, W. E. and Tucker, G. R. *Bilingual Education of Children, the St. Lambert Experiment,* Rowley, Mass.: Newbury House Publishers, Inc., 1972.

Leap, William L. "Grammatical Structure in Native American English: The Evidence from Isleta." Garland D. Bills (Ed.), *Southwest Areal Linguistics,* San Diego State University, Institute for Cultural Pluralism, 1974, p. 180.

Mackey, William F. *Bilingual Education in a Binational School,* Rowley, Mass.: Newbury Publishers, Inc., 1972.

Metcalf, Allan A. "The Study (or Non-Study) of California Chicano English." Garland D. Bills (Ed.), *Southwest Areal Linguistics,* pp. 103-104.

Richardson, Mabel W. "An Evaluation of Certain Aspects of the Academic Achievement of Elementary Pupils in a Bilingual Program: A Project." Mimeographed. Coral Gables, Fla.: The University of Miami, January 1968.

Von Maltitz, Frances. *Living and Learning in Two Languages,* New York: McGraw-Hill, 1975.

IX.

SOCIAL ADJUSTMENT OF INNER-CITY BLACK CHILDREN IN WHITE MIDDLE-CLASS SCHOOLS

By Charles V. Willie

Many school districts throughout the United States have been experimenting with alternative ways of achieving racial balance. Usually school integration programs have been pronounced successful if they result in gains in academic performance for minority students. As important as this may be, public schools must consider the impact of formal education upon the whole child. For this reason, it is important to study the effect, if any, of formal education upon the social adaptation of students as well as its relationship to their academic performance.

Education is concerned with the development of a sense of significance, a sense of control over one's environment and future. It should involve knowledge of theories of justice and how to implement them. And education must develop skills in interpersonal and intergroup relations with individuals of pluralistic cultural backgrounds. Education has to do with these kinds of adaptations, as well as with achievement that is measured by tests of communication and calculation skills.

This chapter presents information from a study of the social adaptations of inner-city black children who were transferred from their predominantly black inner-city schools to middle-class predominantly white elementary schools in a middle-sized urban community for the purpose of achieving a better racial balance. The black children transferred were, of course, in a new situation. Most of them came from families with modest economic resources. Immediately the question comes to mind as to whether the social adaptation of these children was a function of their new situation or their socio-economic and racial backgrounds. To deal with this question, information was obtained on white children new to the same schools because their families had moved recently into the neighborhoods surrounding these schools. Most of the new white children came from middle-class or affluent families.

The study was conducted in a northeastern city in the United States with a population of approximately one quarter of a million people. The elementary and high schools enrolled 45,000 children, 30,000 of whom attended the public schools. At the time of this study, nearly 7 percent of the city-wide population was black. This was the largest racial minority group in the local area.

Prior to this study, the Commonwealth Department of Education directed all school districts to examine racial balances within individual schools and to plan immediate steps to change any racial imbalance.

Two elementary schools in predominantly white middle-class neighborhoods received approximately 155 black children who were deliberately transferred to achieve racial balance. Their combined students numbered about 1470. Blacks bused from the inner-city ghetto raised the proportion of racial minority children to about 10 or 11 percent of all students. Previously, blacks had been only 1 or 2 percent of the students in these schools.

Realizing that social adjustment to a new school setting might be interpreted differently by teachers and students, both were asked to make assessments. The student assessments were self-evaluations of their social adjustment. Two-way assessments on some, but not all, of the students new to these two schools were made. Thus, the study population for black students is 86—slightly more than half of all new black students. They were, however, representative of all blacks newly enrolled.

Of approximately 75 whites new to these schools because their parents recently moved into the surrounding neighborhood, two-way ratings on social adjustment were obtained on 57. They, too, were representative of all newly enrolled whites and served as a comparison group for new black students.

All of the 57 full time teachers in the two schools were white. A child was considered to be socially adjusted if he or she accepted and was accepted by the teachers and pupils of a school. This, more or less, is an operational definition and involves reciprocal actions: acceptance of significant numbers of teachers and pupils by the student; and acceptance of the student by significant numbers of teachers and pupils.

Two different techniques were used to obtain social adjustment ratings. Toward the end of the school year, teachers were given a list of all of their students and were asked to rate each student's level of social adjustment. The homeroom teacher responded to this question: "In your opinion, has each child been assimilated into the school, that is, has each pupil accepted and been accepted by the staff and pupils of this school so that he acts as a part of it?" Teachers checked: *A* for *well assimilated, B* for *fairly well assimilated, C* for *moderately assimilated,* and *D* for *poorly assimilated.* Items *A* and *B* were consolidated into a single category of *well assimilated* for the final analysis.

A student self-rating technique was also used. Children were asked to estimate their social adjustment in school with the assistance of the Colvin Picture Test. In row C of this test pictures are shown of children ranked from 1 to 10. The students were told that picture 10 was that of the least liked boy or girl, and picture 1 that of the most liked person. Each child was asked to pretend the pictures represented students in his or her class, and that he or she should determine his or her position on the continuum of most liked to least liked. The children were instructed to circle the first picture (number 1) if they believed they were least liked, and some other intermediate number if they were neither the least nor the most liked. Responses on the 10-interval scale were grouped into three composite categories for final analysis and designated as *well, moderate,* or *poor social adjustment.* The Colvin Picture Test was administered to all new students except first graders.

A general finding is that elementary school children have the capacity to handle new educational situations well. A majority of the children, blacks and whites, adjusted well to their new school, a judgment supported by the students as well as their teachers. Black children from lower socio-economic inner-city neighborhoods who were bused to predominantly white middle-class schools adjusted well as did white children who were new residents of the middle-class neighborhoods surrounding these schools. From the point of view of the teachers and the students, less than one out of every five of the new students made a poor social adjustment. Eighty percent or more of the new students—including those of different races, socio-economic levels, and residential areas—made good or moderately good social adjustments to their new schools.

While students and teachers were in general agreement about the social adjustment of new students, there was disagreement with reference to particular students. Indeed, there was considerable disagreement between the student's self-assessment and the teacher's assessment of the student's social adjustment to a new school setting. This analysis revealed that students and teachers disagreed one out of every two times. There was only a 51 percent level of agreement between specific black students and their white teachers about the kind of social adjustment each student had made. For judgment about individual white students, there was only a 49 percent level of agreement between the students who made self-assessments and their white teachers. These findings indicate that students and teachers tend to view and evaluate new situations differently and that these differences exist for teachers in relationship to all of their students, including those who are black and those who are white. (See Figures 3 and 4.)

FIGURE 3. THE ADJUSTMENT OF NEW BLACK BUSED CHILDREN TO TWO MIDDLE-CLASS ELEMENTARY SCHOOLS

STUDENT ADJUSTMENT RATINGS	TEACHER RATINGS			TOTAL	
	Well	Moderate	Poor	Number	Proportion
Well	34	10	10	54	.63
Moderate	14	8	3	25	.29
Poor	4	1	2	7	.08
TOTAL Number	52	19	15	86	1.00
Proportion	61	.22	.17		

FIGURE 4. THE ADJUSTMENT OF NEW WHITE NEIGHBORHOOD CHILDREN TO TWO MIDDLE-CLASS ELEMENTARY SCHOOLS

STUDENT ADJUSTMENT RATINGS	TEACHER RATINGS			TOTAL	
	Well	Moderate	Poor	Number	Proportion
Well	24	8	1	33	.58
Moderate	14	3	1	18	.32
Poor	4	1	1	6	.10
Number	42	12	3	57	
TOTAL **Proportion**	.74	.21	.05		1.00

The largest difference between teacher evaluations and student self-evaluations occurred in the determination of poor adjustment. The proportion of black students whom teachers believed were adjusting poorly to their new school was twice as great as the proportion of black students who held a similar belief about themselves. But the porportion of white students who believed that they were adjusting poorly to their new school was twice as great as the proportion of white students of whom teachers held a similar belief. The number of students involved in the analysis of poor adjustment is small, and the conclusions about teachers, therefore, should be accepted as tentative until further studies are conducted.

The discrepancy between the opinions of teachers and the opinions of students was not as great for well adjusted students as it was for poorly adjusted students. Nevertheless, the direction of the discrepancy again is worthy of note for the different racial populations. The proportion of white students whom white teachers believed were well adjusted in their new school was larger than the proportion of white students who believed themselves to be well adjusted. With reference to black students, the proportion whom white teachers believed to be well adjusted was almost the same as the proportion of black students who believed themselves to be well adjusted. Teacher opinion and student opinion came together for the first time in their assessment of well adjusted blacks.

It is interesting to note that the patterns of social adjustment to a new school setting derived from the self-reports of white children in their neighborhood school and inner-city black children who were bused to these predominantly white neighborhoods were similar, almost identical. Sixty-three percent of the black students compared to 58 percent of the white students believed themselves to be well adjusted in their new school; 29 percent of the black students compared to 32 percent of the white students described their social adjustment as moderate; and 8 percent of the black students compated to 10 percent of the white students felt that they were poorly adjusted. The responses of the students indicated that social adjustment of children who are new in school appears to be not a function of race or area of residence, as black and white students of different socio-economic backgrounds made similar self-assessments.

From the perspective of the teachers, however, social adjustment was influenced in a negative way by a black heritage, low-income status, and inner-city residential area. It was also influenced in a positive way by a white heritage, affluent status, and middle-class neighborhood.

The tendency for the white teacher to believe that some black students made a poorer social adjustment to their new school setting than the blacks believed they had made, and that some white students had made a better social adjustment to their new school setting than the whites believed they had made may indicate the persistence of Social Darwinism.

In fact, the teachers ascribed superior adaptation capacities to new white students compared to new black students. Similarity in the self-reports of black and white students meant that their adaptation capacities probably were similar. Yet the teachers persisted in believing that the white affluent new students were more fit in terms of social adjustment than the black inner-city new students.

Presumably, the teachers thought the new white students had made better adaptations since their parents had achieved a higher socio-economic status than had the parents of the new black students.

Charles Darwin's study of the origin of the species demonstrated that those who are fit tend to survive. This had to do with the physical capacity of nonhuman animals. Some social scientists such as William Graham Sumner attempted to apply this theory to human populations for the purpose of explaining social differentiation. They asserted that the more affluent populations in a society are that way because they are more fit, and as such have been able to forge ahead in the struggle for survival.

It is not difficult for people who believe this explanation of the current pattern of social stratification between the races in America to believe that the affluent are superior in all ways, including their capacities to adapt to new situations. Based on this belief, one might assume that middle-class white students would adapt better to a new school setting than working-class or lower-class black children. The teachers apparently made this assumption. Thus, the discrepancy between their assessment of the social adjustment of the black and white new students, and the students' own self-assessment can be characterized as a persisting manifestation of Social Darwinism.

Teachers are said to be acting in accordance with a belief system that distorts reality, since other studies have discovered what has been reported here—that inner-city black children who are bused to schools outside their neighborhood have made good adjustments. During the mid-1960s, Rochester, New York, launched a program that bused inner-city black children to a nearby suburban community consisting largely of middle-class families. The city school administrators described the program as "working well", and they said the children were "benefiting from the experience." Parents who testified at a hearing of the United States Civil Rights Commission said that their children "had adjusted well to school." In Boston, METCO (Metropolitan Council for Educational Opportunities) began a program in 1966 of busing approximately 200 black children from the inner-city to public schools in suburban communities. That program has been in existence for more than a decade and the number of minority children who now participate in it totals more than 2000.

This study of the social adjustment of inner-city black children in white middle-class schools also suggests that one's position and role in an organization or association influences what one sees and how it is interpreted. All should resist the temptation to speak authoritatively for others. It is better that others, blacks and whites, students and teachers, speak for themselves.

Several years ago in an excellent book entitled *Becoming,* Gordon Allport cautioned us to "guard against the fallacy of projecting: of assuming that other people have states of mind, interests, and values precisely like our own." The data presented in this chapter clearly indicate that adults in general, and teachers in particular, should be cautious about speaking for children. Their perceptions of reality may be and often are different.

In summary, one out of every two new students is likely to have a perception of his or her adjustment in an integrated school that differs from the teacher's perception of the adjustment of that particular student. The majority of students, black and white, who are new participants in an integrated school tend to make a good adjustment to their new situation. Self-reports of social adjustment for black and white students who are new participants in integrated schools are similar, indicating that the common experience of being new in a school probably is more significantly related to adjustment than is race, social class, or area of residence. White teachers tend to perceive new middle-class white students as making an adjustment to their integrated school that is better than the adjustment they perceive in new black students from the inner-city and that is better than the white students' own assessment of their social adjustment to the new setting.

REFERENCES

Allport, Gordon. *Becoming.* New Haven: Yale University Press, 1955.

Civil Rights Commission, U.S. *Racial Isolation in the Public Schools.* Washington: U.S. Government Printing Office, 1967.

Hofstadter, Richard. *Social Darwinism in American Thought.* Boston: Beacon Press, 1955.

Sumner, William Graham. *Social Darwinism.* Englewood Cliffs, N. J.: Prentice Hall, 1963.

Teele, James E. *Evaluating School Busing: Case Study of Boston's Operation Exodus.* New York: Praeger, 1973.

Weinberg, Meyer (Ed.). *Integrated Education, A Reader.* Beverly Hills: The Glencoe Press, 1968.

Willie, Charles V. *Race Mixing in the Public Schools.* New York: Praeger, 1973.

X.

URBAN SCHOOL DESEGREGATION

By Robert A. Dentler

Definitions

Applied to public education, the term "to segregate" means to separate, sequester, or isolate students, teachers, staff, and administrators, on the basis of categorical attributes. These attributes could refer to size, shape, color, or any other group as opposed to individual characteristics available to the human imagination. If blue-eyed students were separated from brown-eyed students in classrooms or on playing fields, for example, we would say that segregation was practiced on both "kinds" of students.

Most often, the public attention in the United States is drawn to the isolation of students on the basis of race, which we shall refer to in this essay as ethnicity because the term "race" is too inaccurate to allow intelligent thinking about segregation.

Black Americans have been separated from white Americans within public schools for more than 200 years. More recently, this practice has extended to include Mexican-Americans, American Indians, Puerto Rican Americans, and Oriental Americans, among other ethnic groups. Readers should keep in mind that while we shall focus upon ethnic desegregation of schools, the concept may also be applied to many other categories, ranging from social class to religious group membership, and to mental ability levels and emotional or behavioral characteristics.

On the ethnic dimension, many public schools in the United States are naturally unsegregated, meaning that the children and adults who inhabit them have never been separately assigned or excluded on the basis of ethnic identification. A naturally unsegregated public school is not necessarily a haven of educational or social desirability. It may be a school that is located on the boundary between two or three hostile, mutually antagonistic residential neighborhoods and thus may become a battleground for prejudice and discrimination. Or, it may be a place where good human relations are learned and practiced.

A desegregated public school is one in which policy action has been taken to eliminate student and staff segregation. As with its counterpart, the naturally unsegregated school, the condition of desegregation is not in itself productive of socially or educationally desirable conditions. If the action taken to desegregate has been poorly planned, or if it has been planned to disadvantage one group or another, its outcomes for growth and learning may prove harmful. When courts of law order schools to desegregate, however, agents of justice expect that the action will be designed to be both equitable and educationally beneficial.

Neither an unsegregated nor a desegregated public school is necessarily *integrated*. When the students and staff of a school have achieved integration, we mean that persons within the school interact on the basis of co-equality and not on the basis of categorical distinctions. Many law cases use desegregation and integration interchangeably, but this may be because many lawyers are lacking in sociological sensibilities.

Legal Aspects

Urban school desegregation in the United States cannot be understood without understanding the evolution of public laws. Federal courts have been obligated, ever since passage in 1868 of the 14th Amendment to the Constitution, to apply and interpret that part of the amendment that states, "No State shall...deny to any person within its jurisdiction the equal protection of the laws." This provision, commonly known as the equal protection clause, has become the basis for nearly all court considerations and actions pertinent to school desegregation.

In 1896 the Supreme Court held in *Plessy vs. Ferguson* that a Louisiana law requiring racial segregation of passengers in railway coaches was not racial discrimination, provided the accommodations provided separately were equal. This doctrine of separate-but-equal was applied with few exceptions to every service from passenger railways to public schools in federal court cases from 1896 until 1954. In the 22 years since 1954, when the doctrine was overturned in *Brown vs. Board of Education of Topeka,* the courts have been undoing what they did initially in sanctioning school segregation. While slow and cumbrous in the undoing, the federal judiciary has also been single-minded in its determination to order remedies wherever equal protection is found to have been denied.

The initial Brown decision in 1954, known to lawyers as Brown 1, held that "in the field of public education, the doctrine of 'separate but equal' has no place. Separate educational facilities are inherently unequal." In a 1955 decision known as Brown 2, the court said that "the school authorities have the primary responsibility" for effectuating full compliance with the Brown 1 decision. Brown 2 also directed federal district courts to require school authorities to "make a prompt and reasonable start toward full compliance...to bring about full compliance with all deliberate speed." Courts were also directed to consider and, where necessary, to introduce plans to revise school districts, policies, and practices, to achieve this essential objective.

The Brown decisions and most of the federal decisions that have followed them have concentrated upon de jure as opposed to de facto school segregation. De jure segregation is the result of state (meaning public authority) policies, while de facto segregation refers to the kind that stems from voluntary actions or other circumstances such as private real estate market transactions not governed by public authorities. This distinction has become more and more difficult to maintain as the case law surrounding school segregation has evolved, for there are few ways in which segregation can develop without some state support or failure to exert affirmative action in keeping with the 14th Amendment.

In 1969 the Supreme Court replaced Brown 2 with a unanimous ruling that school districts must end school segregation, not "with all deliberate speed," but at once. This decision ended 14 years of delay, evasion, and trial and error planning in school districts. It introduced a new era in which localities have been ordered to desegregate in as brief a span of time as 18 days, and to do so "root and branch," as the court said, that is, in all schools and at all levels, and in all activities, curricular and extracurricular.

Citizens and educators who continue to resist court-ordered desegregation of public schools often seem to be ignorant of these developments in the history of judicial decisions. As the lay public becomes more aware of that history, however, the attention of those opposed to what they call "forced busing" has shifted to the search for the passage of a constitutional amendment that would reverse the past 22 years of interpretations by the Supreme Court, U.S. Courts of Appeal, and the District Courts.

The Busing Issue: Public Attitudes

Public opinion polls conducted regularly from 1968 through 1974 have disclosed that more than seven out of every ten American citizens say they favor "integrated" public schools, while a greater proportion say they oppose forced busing to achieve school desegregation. A Gallup Poll reported in September, 1974, that 75 percent of whites and 47 percent of blacks favored a constitutional prohibition of busing. The transportation of students by bus is certainly not the issue, for more than 35 percent of all public school children in the nation are currently bused daily to and from school. What, then, is the busing issue?

Part of the opposition is lodged in widespread parental convictions about the desirability of children being able to attend the nearest available neighborhood school facility. Millions of families attempt to occupy housing that is within convenient reach of a public school. Their private consumption preferences are expressed in real estate and in real estate proximity to selected schools. A busing plan relocates school children away from these preferred facilities and toward schools in locations that are *perceived* as alien, distant, or threatening and undesirable.

Another part of the opposition is lodged in the belief that courts are intervening in what is supposed to be local control over local facilities and services. Those opposing busing most vehemently see it as the symbol of their being forced, through the most vulnerable members of their families, to travel, study, eat, play, and interact at places and under conditions that have not been chosen voluntarily. The fact that segregated school assignments are also not voluntary is overlooked.

In his remedial order in the Boston school case, *Morgan vs. Kerrigan,* Federal District Judge W. Arthur Garrity, Jr. illustrated his sensitivity to this attitude when he wrote:

> The court has heard members of the school committee in testimony and others speak against "forced busing" and has received hundreds of letters protesting its use in connection with the state court plan currently in operation. Toward lessening widespread misunderstanding on this point, it may be stated that the court does not favor forced busing. What the plaintiffs seek, and what the law of the land as interpreted by the Supreme Court of the United States commands, is that plaintiffs' right to attend desegregated schools be realized. That right cannot lawfully be limited to walk-in schools. *Swann, supra,* 402 U.S. at 30. If there were a way to accomplish desegregation in Boston without transporting students to schools beyond walking distance, the court and all parties would much prefer that alternative...Boston is simply not a city than can provide its black school children with a desegregated education absent considerable mandatory transportation. No party familiar with the requirements of the law and with the city has ever suggested otherwise.[1]

[1]*Morgan vs. Kerrigan, Memorandum of Decision and Remedial Orders,* June 5, 1975, pp. 56-57. U.S. District Court, District of Mass., Civil Action No. 72-911-G.

At a deeper level, the extent and intensity of public opposition to busing for desegregation concerns the quest for advantageous life chances. Reviewing the best available research evidence, sociologist Nancy St. John, referring to black American and white American urban children, concluded in her book:

> There is probably little difference between the norms of the two groups of children, once social class is controlled, and any differences that exist are certainly not necessarily to the exclusive advantage of one racial group (St. John, 1975, p. 105).

As Nancy St. John goes on to explain, what seems to be the major source of stress varies from social group to social group. Low income families may fear ostracism within the desegregated school setting. Higher income families may fear physical aggression which their children seem poorly prepared to fend off. These and other diverse sources of fear and stress become pooled in sloganized opposition to busing.

The implication here is that American families living in cities and nearby suburbs associate public schooling with the conservation or enhancement of social status. In an economically deprived white, black, or Hispanic enclave, for example, parents may look toward their nearest schools as resources for maintaining whatever level of status security has already been attained by the parents. That security may be negligible, but it has been hard won, and parents may live in the fear of their children losing it.

Upwardly mobile parents in other segregated residential areas may expect that the nearby public schools will facilitate the continuing upward mobility of their children. It may not be literacy and self-development that are cherished so much as a hope of movement upward from one rung on the socio-economic ladder to another, or a hope of protection against downward mobility. This, after all, is how many apologists for public education have extolled the virtues of their services for several generations. And, it is a verified social fact that public schools have for years served to reinforce the stratification system and the income distribution patterns of American urban society.

Sources of Inequality in Schools

Public schools reflect the society whose decision makers create and maintain them. They reinforce the structure and functioning of that society as it is transmitted to upcoming generations of children and youth. In his seminal and provocative book *Inequality*, Christopher Jencks indicated that educational attainment and school achievement alike have a very slight impact upon life chances for a high or a low annual income. Those chances are very largely a product of family socio-economic background. The main effect that schooling does have, however, is to strengthen the input of family background.

In other words, schools tend to operate like sifting and reinforcing mechanisms. Their staffs identify and sift into groups those students who perform, academically and socially, in ways teachers deem appropriate and inappropriate. Students with the most appropriate or "promising" performances are positively reinforced daily and yearly, while others are negatively reinforced through neglect or discipline.

Ray C. Rist demonstrated empirically, in his longitudinal study of elementary classrooms in public schools in St. Louis, that:

> It should be evident from all that has gone before in this study that teachers play the central role in establishing and perpetuating the system of classroom segregation. The consequences and ramifications of this are several. First, teachers create for themselves a paradoxical position. On the one hand, they view themselves as teachers—as those who seek to aid children to learn of themselves and their world. Yet they respond to the socio-economic differences in their students in a way that precludes for some the very opportunity for learning. They generate failure in some of their students while believing themselves to desire success for their charges. The way out of this dilemma for teachers and schools systems in general is to assume that they have done all they can in the face of overwhelming environmental (and genetic) odds (Rist, 1973, p. 246).

Urban white working and middle class parents share the attitudes of teachers who are, after all, their neighbors, friends, and relatives. These adults believe that the children of the minority poor, especially those who are underemployed, unemployed, or on welfare, are children who cannot learn as well as others. There are teachers and parents who do not hold these beliefs, to be sure, but they tend to comprise a minority. Rist is making a generalization, not an indictment.

They believe that the family and neighborhood environments "they" come from make them hostile, cognitively deficient, subject to a low attention span, and poorly motivated to do academic work. Dirty streets, overcrowded and dilapidated homes, and poverty become the badges of educational inferiority, just as they are badges of low status among adults.

The tendency for many boards of education to maintain segregated schools in close tandem with segregated neighborhoods, and to help this tandem along where possible by deliberate policies, is therefore commonplace. Clean streets, expensive homes, and cash incomes become the badges of educational advantage. The best schools, with the best teachers, are located in neighborhoods with these attributes, where the parents and taxpayers also press for advantageous school resources.

Social and economic residential segregation is also inevitably linked with ethnic segregation, for ethnicity is one of the criteria that affect the distribution of life chances for income security in the first place. Where this circularity becomes intentional, de jure school segregation occurs. Where it is broken up by deliberate desegregation, the public clamor concerns far more than inter-ethnic conflict. It concerns a challenge to the very basis of the social structure—socio-economic stratification. The school itself, however, is a vehicle more than a cause in either case.

James Coleman, a sociologist who has researched and consulted on urban school desegregation issues for more than a decade, has recently tried to draw a sharp distinction between the benefits of desegregation when it is carried out "through community actions that involve some consensus among the affected parties, black and white, and the imposition of racial balance by the courts as a constitutional requirement. In my statements about school integration...I have consistently favored the former but not the latter."[2] Coleman's point of view is based upon convictions that he believes are supported by a study he conducted recently and by his earlier work in community conflict theory. His conviction is that the imposition of desegregation generates conflicts which increase rather than decrease ethnic polarities within cities.

His second and more recently researched view is that court imposition of school desegregation on a citywide basis triggers "white flight," a phrase coined in the late 1950s to refer to the out-movement of white households from central cities. Its parallel of black and other minority flight is seldom mentioned. Relatively advantaged white families, he believes, flee to white suburbs, producing more residential segregation which induces deeper segregation of minority children who are left behind.

His first conviction is partially substantiated in the research literature as a whole. Where city and big suburban boards of education have desegregated their public schools willingly and through consensus, the results have been generally beneficial. Unfortunately, the frequency of such occasions is rare. There are not more than 30 non-court or government-ordered desegregated school districts out of more than 500 segregated districts in the nation. Courts, after all, intervene because they offer oppressed ethnic minorities their last resort, years after other types of efforts have failed.

Coleman's second conviction—that court imposed urban school desegregation induces resegregation through white flight—is based upon findings that were contradicted soon after they were made public. One of the most thorough empirical demolitions of his hypothesis is to be found in the work of political scientist Christine Rossell. Her analysis shows that few households relocate to suburbia in order to flee court-ordered desegregation. Rather, Coleman and others of the "white flight" school of thought, confound the normal and longstanding rates of movement from city to suburb with the intervention of the courts. According to the U.S. Bureau of the Census in 1971, about 80 percent of the net population increase in the nation from 1960 to 1970 took place in metropolitan areas; however, 98.5 percent of this growth occurred outside of central cities, in suburbs. Most exponents of the white flight thesis fail to take this great rate of change, which is unrelated to court orders of any kind, into adequate account. The latter is a short-term, one-time event. Among the white households that do relocate, moreover, as a result of court desegregation of schools, many return to the city within a two- to three-year period.

[2]*Phi Delta Kappan,* November 1975, p. 169.

One complication in both of Coleman's arguments stems from a tendency to lump demographically different types of cities into a single sample. Many cities were becoming mainly black settlements years before school desegregation became an issue.

In fact, nearly half of the black American population was, in 1969, concentrated in 50 central cities. A third was located in 15 cities out of the 50. Six cities had black majorities: Washington, Compton, East St. Louis, Newark, Gary, and Atlanta. Eight cities, including Baltimore, New Orleans, Savannah, Detroit, Birmingham, Richmond, St. Louis, and Jackson, had populations that were from 40 to 50 percent black.

Where the black student enrollments in a district exceed two thirds, the effect of court-imposed desegregation is potentially to induce resegregation, for these are districts in which the white population has long since gone suburban. In such situations, *metropolitan* area desegregation is the most viable solution to the problem. It is just a matter of time before urban-suburban school desegregation plans in some of the nation's 100 largest metropolitan areas will become fairly commonplace. Louisville, Kentucky, represents the trend in this regard, although there are other such plans in effect in the Deep South. Currently, a Supreme Court decision limits the prospect of court-imposed metropolitan desegregation, but this issue continues to be tested in the federal courts.

Where black and other minority enrollments in combination are smaller than, or approximately equal to, the white student enrollments, school resegregation is extremely unlikely. In cities of this type, from San Francisco to Boston, the Supreme Court dictum that public schools should be neither black nor white, but "just schools," is completely achievable. In many other cities, where black, Hispanic, and Oriental students comprise less than one third of the enrollments, no resegregation prospect can be argued. Federal court imposition of school desegregation in Minneapolis, is indicative of this condition.

Planning

As with any other substantial change in social policy, urban school desegregation can be well planned or poorly planned, depending upon local capabilities and intentions. The quality of planning has strong consequences for the quality of the outcomes for students, with respect to equal protection and to educational benefits. The outcomes become the index of quality both in planning and in implementation.

Sociologist Richard Boardman, for example, found that a desegregation plan which was hastily drawn up by inexperienced locals in one New England city, failed to involve either teachers or parents in the planning process. As a result of faulty reassignment procedures, failure to co-plan with knowledgeable parties, and other kinds of deficiencies, all three groups of students showed significant declines in reading and mathematics achievement scores over a two-year period. These were the children who were transferred, those who remained in place, and those in the receiving schools.

Many barriers to good planning are present in most segregated urban school systems: agents of the system are themselves products and defenders of the status quo. They often plan against their will and from a base of ignorance about objectives. Federal funds and foundation grants were invested in the mid-1960s in developing institutes and centers where expertise in desegregation planning could be trained, but rising public opposition prevented the growth of these units. By now, many lawyers have had professional experience with school desegregation, but very few of them are knowledgeable urbanists or students of public education.

Judges expect planning proposals to be presented to them by parties to suits. When these are patently unacceptable, they must on occasion do the planning themselves. They are generally ill equipped by training or by staff limitations to undertake this task. In increasing numbers, judges have retained independent experts to assist them, but the supply of such individuals is extremely small.

In addition, in the course of planning, countless other defects in urban school systems are brought to light. If good planning is to be accomplished, these must also be remedied; but there are severe limits on the extent to which these can be treated if they are not linked plainly to the wrong of segregation, which is the crucial defect to be remedied.

The enormous dilemmas in planning effectively has been explored in detail for at least two cities, New York and Boston. In the Boston case, the planning problem as it exists for hundreds of American cities can be seen to have been pivotal to the generation of early conflicts and failures in the total process.

Federal Judge W. Arthur Garrity, Jr. found the public schools to have been deliberately segregated in an opinion he delivered in June, 1974. At that time, the Boston School Committee had no plan for desegregating its schools. It had refused directives from the State Board of Education to prepare and execute such a plan since late in 1965. The State Board had therefore developed a short term plan on its own and without help or the provision of vital information from local agencies, as early as 1972. In lieu of other planning options, Judge Garrity ordered the implementation of the state plan for September, 1974, and called for local preparation of a permanent plan by December 16, 1975.

The state plan was defective in several respects. It did not affect roughly half of the schools in the system because it was drawn to conform to a state statute. Administration and teacher personnel were not included in the plan. Redistricting was complex and difficult for the public to comprehend. In the part of the city known as South Boston, students were assigned to what the plan termed the South Boston High School Complex, which consisted of an old high school facility plus a converted bath house by the sea, two converted elementary schools, and the formerly all-black Roxbury High School. Local reaction to this latter aspect of the plan was extremely negative. Conflicts developed around this complex which have continued for more than a year, even beyond the period of its implementation.

When December 16, 1974, arrived, the Boston School Committee reviewed and rejected a plan devised by its own local staff—a staff which had no prior experience in such planning. Judge Garrity considered jailing and fining the committee members who had voted against their own plan. Instead, at their request, he gave them until January 27, 1975, to submit a revised plan to the court. The School Committee then retained the same local planners from its own staff to contradict their previous work and, in one month, to prepare a new plan for desegregating 190 schools serving 75,000 students.

Simultaneously, Judge Garrity appointed a Panel of Masters and two Experts to review these and other plans from other parties to the case. Although Judge Garrity had presided over *Morgan vs. Hennigan,* the liability phase, and *Morgan vs. Kerrigan,* the remedy phase, for two years at this point, he had received no professional help save from his one law clerk! The advent of the masters and the experts enabled him to turn his attention to his 1600 other federal cases for two months.

Early in April, the masters submitted a report to Judge Garrity. In it, they rejected all of the plans that had been submitted by the parties as either unconstitutional or technically undesirable, and they presented a plan of their own devising. It contained features drawn from the work of the parties, of course. The Judge reviewed and amended this plan slightly and filed his order on May 10. He was aided in this modification by the two experts, who continued to assist him.

Planning Educational Improvements

After witnessing a decade of failure and struggle, Judge Garrity was determined to issue a plan that would fulfill the essential objective of equal protection and one that would reverse decades of inferior education for all children in Boston. Like the Denver and Minneapolis desegregation plans that went before it, his plan encompassed far more than the mechanics of redistributing students and staff, for no mere assignment scheme would conceivably remedy the wrongs suffered by the clients of the Boston School Committee.

In his introduction to the plan, Judge Garrity wrote:

> In the court's quest for a remedy adequate to reviving the vision of an equitable and effective public school system, it has planned for schools that will be free, universal, inclusive, and sound in ways that meet the educational needs and aspirations of all of Boston's citizens. It believes that the reconstruction o the ideal of the Common School requires a common concern with equality and excellence throughout all institutions and groups in the entire Greater Boston area.[3]

[3]*Morgan vs. Kerrigan, op. cit.,* p. 4.

Consistent with these aims, his plan encompassed every school facility and educational program within the system. It closed permanently about 30 facilities which were found to be unfit and unsafe for school use. It redistricted the entire system, at all levls. One of the new districts was designed as a citywide magnet school district, which parents could apply to have their children attend out of enthusiasm for a quality desegregated program of instruction—in other words, a voluntary subsystem.

His plan required the provision of special educational services in all schools for handicapped and other students with special needs, physical, emotional, or cognitive. It required bilingual instruction in six foreign languages for students whose native languages were other than English. It established a new and firm administrative chain of command, provided a basis for decentralization of the curriculum, and facilitated student and parent participation in governance.

It also accepted pledges from 23 colleges and universities, 100 cultural institutions such as museums and centers for the arts, and 16 businesses and labor groups, to support and assist the public schools in the development of educational excellence. These pledges were incorporated into the order and the School Committee's acceptance of this support was made subject to continuing jurisdiction. It also required profound revisions in occupational and vocational education programs throughout the city and the physical repair and renovation of facilities. Finally, it required the School Committee to hire and retain staff to carry out these plans at all levels, and it set a timetable for implementation.

In all likelihood, desegregation plans formulated during the remainder of the 1970s, whether for metropolitan areas or for single urban and suburban districts, will reflect very similar concerns for desegregation within a context of educational reform. The Boston plan, like its Denver and Minneapolis predecessors, gives a concrete and positive answer to the question: busing for what? The answer will become, busing for fulfillment of the Fourteenth Amendment, which stipulates equal access to learning *opportunities* that are worthy of the term.

Implementation

Poor planning generates poor educational outcomes, but good planning poorly executed can be equally harmful. Again, as Coleman has noted, "One of the peculiarities of the whole desegregation period has been the lack of interest by advocates on both sides in making a desegregated system work successfully."[4] Often, the same school board members and their staffs who willfully created a segregated system are assigned the task of implementing a desegregation plan. Not only are these persons apt to "be of the same opinion still," they are also, by virtue of long conditioning, unable to modify their own policies and practices.

The southern desegregation experience suggests that, short term, say for a period of four to five years, the process of implementation is balky, bumbling, and diversionary. Where the planning quality is good, however, and where monitoring and jurisdiction are well maintained, the long term outcomes become positively beneficial. The combined force of the law and planning prescription is considerable, under conditions where courts or other authoritative agents of justice remain vigilant and insistent. School segregation usually takes decades to mature. We cannot expect its wrongs will be undone overnight.

Again, the Boston case illustrates the short term process and offers clues to the long term outcomes. The court order was published on May 10, 1975. By July, some administrators had formed an Office of Implementation within the system. But by December, the School Committee had still not established a table of administrative reorganization, a budget, and a personnel roster and pay scale, essential to legitimizing and stabilizing this little unit. Two high schools in the system were in sporadically violent turmoil during the fall, but the system failed to appoint a director of school security. When the court insisted on an appointment within one week during November, the School Committee appointed its chief custodial engineer and the court intervened and nullified the appointment as inappropriate.

Gradually, however, the Office of Implementation took hold. Its personnel complement expanded from six to thirty between June and December. It obtained good office space and some equipment. It established reasonably effective communications with all parts of the system, and began to coordinate most aspects of fulfillment of the court order. External to the system, the court utilized monitors within problem schools, the Community Relations Service of the U.S. Department of Justice, U.S. Marshalls, and an appointed Citywide Coordinating Council with a full time staff, as resources for implementation. In addition, it retained the services of the two experts.

Even more gradually, over a period of several years, the plan will become the determinant of the policies and the educational practices of the school system as a whole. The implications of the court order will expand, not narrow, as a new subsystem of vocational instruction is adopted, as magnet programs come to be sought after by parents for their unique merits, as special educational services are perfected, and above all, as the experience of attending an ethnically mixed facility outside of one's immediate neighborhood becomes utterly commonplace. In this future condition many teachers will also be liberated from the old

[4]*Phi Delta Kappan, op. cit.,* p. 169.

constraints of socio-economic and ethnic differentiation. They will do less sifting and more positive reinforcing and individualizing of all instruction. Their ability to do this will hinge upon the attitudes and expectations of the public at large, of course. But as minority youths gain entry to the previously exclusive high schools, the myths of educability will change.

Achievement Outcomes

The research evidence bearing on the question of whether school desegregation affects the school achievement levels of students is mixed. In his comprehensive review of that evidence, historian Meyer Weinberg found that for the most part, desegregation improves the achievement of minority students and does not harm that of white students.[5] Sociologist Nancy St. John, summarizing the results of 120 studies of this question to date, was less hopeful than Weinberg:

> But although desegregation is not to date a demonstrated success, it is not yet a demonstrated failure. There is as little evidence of consistent loss as there is of consistent gain. Further, in spite of the large number of studies, various limitations in design weaken the best of them. Thus in a sense the evidence is not all in.[6]

What both Weinberg and St. John neglect to stress very strongly is that desegregation research from 1955 to 1970 was, of necessity, dependent upon plans and the implementation of plans that were comparatively devoid of educational design. In other words, the question whether desegregation benefits student achievement should properly only be tested in the context of a plan where such benefits have been built into the intended changes.

Equal protection under law is important in its own right for purposes of the learning and humanization that result from the advent of justice. But equal protection, even when it aims at equalizing initial opportunities for school achievement, has *no* necessary or predictive relation to reading comprehension and mathematical or scientific literacy. Only now is it becoming commonplace to make such connections a part of desegregation planning as such. There are exceptions, to be sure, especially in school districts that have chosen to desegregate without court intervention. But, the cases of Denver, Minneapolis, and Boston, have altered the old pattern of emphasis upon student reassignment alone, to the neglect of other concerns.

[5]Meyer Weinberg, *Desegregation Research: An Appraisal,* 2nd Edition, Bloomington, Ind.: Phi Delta Kappa, 1970.

[6]Nancy St. John, *School Desegration Outcomes for Children,* John Wiley and Sons, 1975, p. 120.

In addition, researchers have been somewhat narrow in their approaches to the effects of desegregation. Most often, they have relied upon concepts of positive and negative effects resulting from changs in social learning and self-concept, as these are impacted by changes in the scope of socio-economic and ethnic group interactions. The concept is expressed in its simplest form by Coleman:

> The research results indicate that a child's performance, especially a working-class child's performance, is greatly benefited by his going to school with children who come from educationally strong backgrounds... A child's learning is a function more of the characteristics of his classmates than of those of his teacher.[7]

The concept does *not* mean that children learn more algebra or geography from each other than from the teacher. It means that school learning takes place within classroom peer groups and that the level of learning in a group reflects a contextual effect. The effect is assumed to be mediated through individual identification with the group, so that aspirations and self-expectations are raised for socio-economically and ethnically disadvantaged learners through social contact, social comparison, and identification. The mediation can be swamped and negated, according to the concept, if too many disadvantaged learners are included within the group.

Research influenced by this perspective tends to approach the question of the achievement outcomes of desegregation with the prior assumption that the purpose of desegregation is to mix an educationally suitable small number of lower status, minority students with a suitably large number of higher status, majority students. There is enough validity to the principle of contextual effect so that when such a mix occurs, minority achievement does indeed increase, at least slightly.

This approach is then used in reverse, to explain the absence of achievement effects, and even to guide policy by indicating that desegregation is worthwhile when there are enough "eager achievers" from the white middle-class available as a pool into which to place black lower-class, non-achievers. The upshot in such research is selective inattention to the effects of teacher behavior, the design of instruction, and planful upgrading of the curriculum. The upshot in policy guidance is an argument against urban desegregation under conditions where part of the white middle class has relocated to suburbia.

Final Comment

Future research into urban school desegregation will be broader-based than the research conducted to date. Future research will examine

[7]*Phi Delta Kappan, op. cit.,* p. 163.

overall structural effects of desegregation, much as Christine Rossell's study, cited earlier in this essay, has tried to do. Such research will ask whether the conditions under which school learning takes place have been improved as a result of planful, well implemented desegregation. It will not assume that schools, as they are conventionally organized, are instruments of powerful influence upon achievement, in the presence or absence of desegregation policies. Rather, such research will seek out instances where, as a result of desegregation, the processes of urban schooling have been modified in ways that benefit all students.

It is possible that a well-planned desegregation effort could improve physical facilities, increase and improve the quality of citizen participation, stabilize and give new hope to classroom teachers, and above all, equalize the distribution of learning opportunities, and *still* manifest negligible effects upon school achievement. This would not signify that desegregation as a policy had failed or succeeded. It would signify, instead, that the applied science of educational research and development has a long way to go before it speaks pertinently to the factors that produce effective teaching and learning.

What school desegregation does when it is well planned and executed is to break the widespread public assumption that academic ability is a predictable outcome of the social and genetic accident of birth. When parents, taxpayers, teachers, and students are released from having to behave as if this myth is true—thereby helping make it come true—then we can concentrate as a society on the quest for the kinds of public instruction that make a positive difference for all children.

Planful desegregation does far more than cut holes in the enclaves of educational advantage that are tucked away in corners of our major cities. Planful desegregation ventilates the entire system of public education. It exposes to the sunlight the educationally sterile, if socially gratifying, schools within poor white neighborhoods. It liberates black and other minority children and their teachers from dilapidated, fire-unsafe dungeons, inside the aging ghettoes. It mobilizes the institutions of the city at large to pay attention to the needs of the very young. Its occasion generates new necessities, which breed new and inventive programs of service to the young, proving again that education is too precious a process to be stored in isolated classrooms. Above all, desegregation communicates to children and youth that the rule of law continues and is extended to include them.

Future desegregation research will transcend concern with conventional measures of achievement; and will deal with the total span of effects in ways that inform the quest for effectiveness in educating the young.

REFERENCES

Boardman, Richard P. *A Comparison of the Academic Performance and Achievement of Fifth and Sixth Grade Pupils in a Program of Pupil Transfer.* Columbia University, Teachers College, doctoral thesis, 1967.

Boston Bar Association. *Desegregation: The Boston Orders and their Origin.* Boston, August 1975.

Coleman, James S. "Racial Segregation in the Schools: New Research with New Policy Implications." *Phi Delta Kappan,* October 1975, pp. 75-78.

Commonwealth of Massachusetts Board of Education. *Short Term Plan to Reduce Racial Imbalance in the Boston Public Schools.* Boston, November 1972.

Community Conflict. Glencoe, Ill.: Free Press, 1958.

Dentler, Robert A. and Scott, Marvin B. "Boston School Desegregation and Boston University: Plans and Prospects." *Debate and Understanding,* Vol. 1, No. 1, Boston University, Martin Luther King Center, 1975.

The Desegregation Packet. Massachusetts Research Center, 3 Joy Street, Boston, Mass., 02108.

Jencks, Christopher. *Inequality: A Reassessment of the Effect of Family and Schooling in America.* New York: Basic Books, 1972.

Rist, Ray C. *The Urban School: A Factory for Failure.* Cambridge, Mass.: M.I.T. Press, 1973, p. 246.

Rogers, David. *New York City and the Politics of School Desegregation.* Center for Urban Education, July 1968.

St. John, Nancy. *School Desegregation: Outcomes for Children.* New York: John Wiley and Sons, 1975, p. 105.

XI.

INTEGRATION OF AMERICAN SOCIETY
By Marvin B. Scott

American Minorities

America is a nation of immigrants and their descendants. The first immigrants were those we call American Indians. They journeyed to this continent many, many years before the arrival of white immigrants and numbered in the millions at the time the first settlers landed from England. The early English settlers came to this country in search of religious freedom and economic opportunities. Aided by the Indians in the initial adaptation to an unsettled country, they gradually became more successful in building a life here.

In the more than three hundred years since the beginning of white immigration, there have been periodic waves of new and different immigrants. Each new group faced exploitation by another as earlier arrivals looked down on and exploited the most recent arrivals. The largest group of recent immigrants are the Puerto Ricans, who face monumental problems in attempting to be assimilated into American culture. In a sense the Puerto Ricans have become the newest group to be exploited by the society which they wish to enter. But one group, in strong contrast to the others, was brought to American involuntarily, by force, stripped of its past culture, and generally looked down on by all:

the blacks.

Economic necessity, the combination of sheer survival and yearning for materials success, has always played a major part in shaping the minority centers of America. These same realities have greatly affected the mobility of various groups within the country. As new immigrants to America fought for survival and for upward mobility, and as technology struggled to keep up with the American dream, increasing emphasis was placed on technical skills. Often the menial tasks that once consumed the lives of many Americans were transformed, but different menial tasks appeared. New immigrants inherited a large portion of new menial tasks. Each succeeding group of immigrants started off on the lowest rungs of the economic and social ladders, and gradually worked up to a position of security on both.

But all groups have not been equally successful in climbing these ladders. Neither have all members of each group found the same degree of success. In many cases, the choice was not up to the group or to the individuals within that group. Skin color has often been given as a reason for lack of economic success: a certain person is inadequate because of the color of his skin, or so some think. Thus, the black American was not allowed to share in the American dream for over three centuries. To this day the black American still experiences a lack of equal opportunity in a number of areas, even to the point of not having easy access to many public institutions.

Factors influencing all people are often overridingly economic. If a white child, of whatever ethnic background, is hungry, and a black child is hungry; both children share real hunger and the same socio-economic status. If they are both tempted to steal an apple from a fruit stand then these two children have more in common than those who have the same skin color but who face different economic situations. These two children will act in the same way because both are seeking relief from hunger.

Traditionally America has encouraged the uniqueness of the individual and has prided itself on being a melting pot of all groups. Today, the assimilation trend is changing. Distinct ethnic groups, realizing the value of their ethnic heritage, are claiming a separate identity and taking pride in ethnicity. This identification with an ethnic heritage is a new experience for some. Others, however, have stayed within their immigrant groups, and maintained at least in part, customary patterns of living according to old-country ways while building a life in a new country. Much of this ethnic clumping is centered on religious beliefs and common work.

Thus, America is dotted with small enclaves of various ethnic groups. This separateness has led to many of the problems facing school systems today. Schools are trying to integrate a population which has resisted integration for more than 200 years. Can we really refer to America as a melting pot? A more valid description today would be to call it a mixed salad; the bowl is filled with many different things which are then tossed. The various items in the salad are mixed but not blended.

It is important to the future of this country that the concept of ethnicity continue; a sharing of traditions and customs will strengthen our social fabric. However, ethnicity must be tempered in both school and society so as to support the positive aspects of each culture and encourage all groups to share in the richness of other cultures.

The American Majority

The majority of Americans today are faced with national questions which seem quite different from those raised during the sixties when the cry for social consciousness was on the lips of our youth. Surrounded by extremely uncertain economic conditions as well as by global problems of increasing population, decreasing natural resources, and ever present pollution, our citizens seem to be driven to a more self-centered form of daily living.

Who are the majority of Americans? What are their interests and what are their expectations for their children? George Wallace refers to them as the little man or the forgotten people of America. They appear to be middle Americans, those who earn from 12 to 20 thousand dollars a year. They seemingly do not have enough money to individually influence big business nor are they poor enough to always be disgruntled about the system. Singly they do not exist; collectively they possess a tremendous buying power in the society. The group is typically church-going and usually law-abiding, although it tends to interpret the law as a protection for its capitalistic ambitions rather than something that applies to them personally. Portions of the law do not apply to them, for example, as each year businesses lose millions to employee thefts.

These citizens are protective and defensive. They tend to feel threatened when people who are different infringe on their way of life; whether by moving next door or demanding equal educational opportunities. Many members of this group view their economic survival as marginal. Therefore they are apt to focus on survival as their dominating personal interest. Any individual whom they fear will either bring down their property value or threaten their childrens' future by diminishing the quality of education offered in their schools, is very definitely an outsider and, as such, a possible enemy.

President Ford has said this country is a nation of immigrants and that no group has a monopoly on the resources of the land. It is essential for all Americans to unite in addressing the fundamental needs of our nation. But before the majority of Americans are imbued with the ideas and ideals on which our country was founded some formidable obstacles will have to be overcome.

Genetics and Race

This essay will not deal with all the factors that contribute to discrimination and racial tensions. But a brief consideration of some highly publicized contentions will indicate some of the difficulties faced by minorities and proponents of equal access.

For many years it has been held by some that people of color were genetically inferior to whites. The debate has raged in many quarters and has plagued those who would take an active stand in the field of equal rights. The question, on the surface, is not worthy of debate. It is important, however, to know something about the work of Arthur Jensen and Richard Herrnstein. Professor Herrnstein's research places those who do menial work into lower intelligence categories and concludes that children born into working class families have virtually no chance of moving up in socio-economic status. Yet many who do menial work are suffering from a lack of exposure to education due to the denial of their rights of equal access. Years of this denial may assure a lack of education, and this lack will not be overcome in a generation or two. But this is a social and environmental circumstance. Evidence that those who do menial work are genetically inferior has not been established. One must recognize that even at birth the child has been influenced by hereditary factors (genetics), by possible mutations which occurred during early cell division (innate), by experiences in the uterus (congenital), and by conditions during the birth process (constitutional). Thus, even in the first weeks of life, many non-environmental factors other than genetics have helped shape infants. Add to this the later insults to the human organism and pervasive environmental factors and there is little wonder that these children fail to improve their status.

Professor Jensen, in a controversial article, contends that minorities, specifically black children, may not be endowed with the same intelligence level as white children when comparisons are made by using standardized IQ tests. A weakness in his argument is that IQ test results may not be valid because the samples used in the studies reported were based on white, middle-class norms.

The great danger in these arguments is not so much in the views themselves, but in the prejudices they seem to uphold. Progress toward equal education has been retarded by the inappropriate uses of the Jensen and Herrnstein arguments by those who would deny equal access to education.

Why Integration

The Liberty Bell is inscribed with the inscription: "Proclaim liberty throughout all the land, unto all the inhabitants thereof.'' But this philosophy has not extended to all Americans. The races are still segregated in many ways and many places. This nation was founded on the ideal of equality for all: where did the dream go wrong, and how is it repairable if it is in need of repair? Some suggest that dwindling resources will force people to accept one another more. Others cynically propose that all minorities will occupy some type of reservation, such as large city ghettos or Indian reservations.

Our laws and our heritage state that all persons have equal access to the resources of this nation and that the rights of others are not to be infringed upon. Therefore, it is vitally important not to subvert the minds and wills of others. It is frightening to think that when a child is denied a good education because of racial hatred, he or she will not attain full use of his or her capabilities or make an appropriate contribution to society.

Justice requires an integrated society. This author does not define an integrated society as one that simply has blacks and whites working side by side or, in instances such as busing for education, experiencing a forced relationship between the two groups. Integration is a more involved condition in which the groups live together, work together, and totally interact within the society to improve the condition of all. Integration is a concept that assumes we are a unified people with several common goals and that America is a healthy place in which to live and to raise children.

The Law

It is assured under the 14th Amendment of the Constitution that all citizens of the United States shall have equal protection under the law. the *Brown vs. Board of Education of Topeka* (1954) Supreme Court ruling found that segregated public schools are not "equal" and cannot be made "equal," and that hence they deprived citizens of the equal protection of the laws. Any infringement on this right of citizens is subject to adjudication under federal law. Despite this constitutional assurance many Americans are still struggling to achieve this protection. Since the mid-nineteenth century, blacks in this country have been systematically denied access to public facilities. A few states prevented equal education under the separate but equal doctrine. This concept was finally struck down by the *Brown vs. Board of Education of Topeka* decision, but equal educational opportunity for all is still unrealized. As vocational training unions and other labor organizations exclude people of one ethnic group as opposed to another, they make it difficult and often impossible for some ethnic groups to secure training and subsequent employment requiring such training. School boards that refuse to integrate schools and continue to deny equal access to education are in violation of the law. Such boards are more and more frequently being superceded by courts and court-appointed authorities to assure that schools will be run in accordance with the law of the land.

Education as a Frontier of Integration

Education has been regarded as an equalizer of all men. However, some have called it a subversive act because it exposes students to new, sometimes revolutionary, and often biased ideas. When an educator uses the classroom to promote bias, instill prejudicial attitudes, and incite learners, it is subversive. However, the learner can be no more influenced than the teacher's presentations permit. Unfortunately, there are persons in our society who appear to think that they possess, by virtue of race or national origin, greater access to "truth" and more right to the free commodity of education than do others.

Education is one of the greatest resources that our country possesses. It has led to the present level of advanced scholarship and sophisticated technology. Education must be informed by facts that are progressive and established by precedents; not just based on case studies. It must be committed to the pursuit of truth. Education has been the key to upward mobility of minorities and all people in America for generations. It has been, and is, the common ground where ideas are explored, knowledge shared, and skills acquired. This is an exciting idea—that education can serve as the key to upward mobility. It would seem, therefore, to be the best possible frontier of integration.

But education has also become a focus of controversy and dissent. Schools are faced with having to take on ideas which have been relinquished or reduced by other institutions or by parents themselves. Morals and sex instruction is, in a number of cases, out of the hands of parents and in the hands of teachers. The fiercest battles, however, relate to race and the integration of society. The next few paragraphs will describe some of the issues around which battle lines have been drawn.

Busing

Busing has become the lightning rod for protestors. In the fall of 1975 the U.S. Senate attempted to pass a bill which stated that busing to achieve integrated school systems consumed too much energy and should therefore be abandoned. The issue, of course, is not really how much gasoline is used; the issue is whether or not integration will take place in schools.

In order to truly begin the process of integration, it is imperative that children of all kinds be placed in close proximity to each other. A broad and tolerant awareness should result from children sharing experiences and playing and working together. Busing is a means toward achieving this end. The question is not busing, but rather, will there be integration?

Quotas

Should quotas be established to determine the number and kinds of children to be bused in order to achieve integration? This is a question for which no firm answer has been proposed. Should blacks be included in a given school system in proportion to their representation in the total population? Should institutions of higher learning limit the number of qualified white students who are admitted in order to make room for a quota of minority students?

It is hoped that the best qualified in any situation will be selected. The question is not who is qualified but who is best qualified, and obviously at this time in history it is easier to find qualified whites than blacks. Education and educators must strive to prepare the best qualified, irrespective of race or creed or color. It is essential now to give individuals who have not been included in the mainstream a chance to compete and achieve. The use of quotas will at least increase the number of educational and vocational opportunities available to minorities.

Integrated Education

Tools and techniques for achieving integrated education are slowly being developed. History books are beginning to document the contributions and achievements of the various minorities. Textbooks now show people of all races smiling, enjoying life, and expressing positive images. Instructors, although hired on a quota basis, are presenting images of minority teachers to children all over the country. But this is only a beginning. The formation of an integrated society with a new and healthy respect for others will proceed slowly.

What Price for Integration

Changing a whole school so that integration can be achieved is an expensive process. How can American cities support these costs? This is another question for which no answer has been found as yet. The tax base of many of these cities has eroded as the white middle-class continues to move to the suburban areas. Many cities have generated tax revenues from the large companies which have downtown offices or factories, but now a number of these companies are moving out too. Declining populations and reduced funds have forced some large cities to the brink of financial collapse. The poor and the unemployed in the cities obviously cannot compensate for the loss of the middle-class and the large companies. In some cities commuter taxes, assessed on those who don't live in the city, have generated additional income but not enough to finance vital services. Those who move out of the city only postpone a confrontation with the problem. People in the suburbs, as well as those in the cities will pay the price of quality education. Each child should receive the same amount of investment in his education, whether he lives in a privileged area of the suburbs or a neglected area of the city.

Massive amounts of federal and other expenditures are needed in order to meet the educational needs of tomorrow. It is also important to provide support to both public and private colleges and universities. These institutions have made significant contributions to the public interest. We need many things to achieve integration, and one of the most important is the leadership which can be provided by public and private institutions of higher learning.

Integrated Education and the Year 2000

Education today does not necessarily provide job security, neither does it always render a person competent to deal with the problems of this highly technological society. At best, the schools provide minimal skills and notions on how to learn. In the future the process of acquiring an education will become much more automated and will be supplemented by machines and devices that substantially change the role of the teacher. The use of so-called smart drugs to improve memory or attention could greatly influence the rate of learning in children.

As industry becomes more mechanized and the work week is decreased, there will be more free time available to many people. Recreation will continue to grow as a major industry as people seek things to do. University curricula will reflect this increased leisure time as more and more citizens seek more advanced education.

Teachers will be greatly affected by the concept of accountability, wherein the teacher is accountable to the public for his or her delivery of educational services. If a student is judged capable of learning and the teacher fails to deliver to the student, then the teacher will be held liable. We may well see an increase in the number of law suits based on teacher competence or incompetence.

Tenure will be a thing of the past. A teacher will instead receive a multi-year contract, as opposed to a guaranteed job for a professional lifetime, which is the current practice. Today the teacher is provided a free place to practice his or her profession at the taxpayer's expense. I suspect that teachers some day may have to rent facilities from school officials in order to practice their profession. Implicit in this is that teachers' salaries will increase substantially above levels of inflation.

Teachers will have to become educational diagnosticians. They will have to identify by observation given behavior patterns and provide for the student the proper learning programs in order to assure his or her learning to capacity. There are many styles of learning. Open classroom teaching is not good for all children, and neither is the traditional classroom. Some students learn better in one than the other. Therefore, those and all other options must be available so that each student can have the greatest chance to learn. The use of standardized tests may see increased use for a number of years, simply because the system in its present state is unable to cope with the numbers of students. Our education systems will learn from countries such as India and Japan, which have learned to deal with large groups of students.

The year 2000 can roll in with great promise or it can mark an educational decline. Our youth will need to have an appreciation of others as well as a more complete understanding of themselves, and they must be able to relate to their environment in an effective manner. If they possess this understanding and these skills, they can become effective citizens of their country. Integrated schools, offering quality education, will make it possible for our youth to be effective citizens in the twenty-first century.

REFERENCES

Alexander, Kern and Solomon, Erwin S. *Brown vs. Board of Education of Topeka, College and University Law,* The Michie Company, Charlottesville: 1972, pp. 558-562.

Herrnstein, Richard. "IQ." *The Atlantic,* Vol. 228, No. 3, pp. 43-58, 63, 64.

Jensen, Arthur R. "How Much Can We Boost IQ and Scholastic Achievement?" *Harvard Educational Review,* 1969, Vol. 39, Nos. 1-123, p. 70.

____. "The Heritability of Intelligence." *The Saturday Evening Post,* 1972, Vol. 244, pp. 8-10.

93   2

This book was composed with Greylock's in-house Compugraphic Unified Composer® editing terminal and Unisetter® phototypesetter. The text typeface is English Times and the titles and headings appear in Paladium.

DATE DUE

MAY 10 '79	MAY 2 '79		
GAYLORD			PRINTED IN U.S.A